Is The Antichrist Alive and Well?

10 keys to his identity

ED HINDSON

HARVEST HOUSE PUBLISHERS
Eugene, Oregon 97402

Cover by Terry Dugan Design, Minneapolis, Minnesota

IS THE ANTICHRIST ALIVE AND WELL?
Copyright © 1998 Ed Hindson
Published by Harvest House Publishers
Eugene, Oregon 97402

Library of Congress Cataloging-in-Publication Data
Hindson, Edward E.
      Is the antichrist alive and well? / Ed Hindson.
         p. cm.
      Includes biographical references.
      ISBN 1-56507-833-0
      1. Antichrist. 2. Antichrist—Biblical teaching. 3. Bible—Prophecies—Antichrist.
I. Title.
BT985.H55 1998
236-dc21   98-22645
                                                        CIP

Printed in the United States of America

98 99 00 01 02 03 / BO / 10 9 8 7 6 5 4 3 2 1

*To those great servants of God
who have resisted the
spirit of the Antichrist in our generation:
James Dobson
Jerry Falwell
James Kennedy*

Acknowledgments

I want to thank several of my friends and colleagues for their advice and suggestions on this present study. I am especially grateful to Ed Dobson, Mal Couch, Thomas Ice, Randall Price, J. Dwight Pentecost, and John Walvoord for their helpful suggestions. I also want to express my gratitude to my administrative assistant, Mrs. Emily Boothe, who typed the original manuscript and to my wife, Donna, whose encouragement made this study possible.

Contents

The Shadow of Coming Events

All of us are curious about the future. There is something in human nature that wants to know what is going to happen in the days ahead. God speaks to that need in our lives by revealing the future before it happens. Bible prophecies give us a glimpse of things to come. We aren't given all the details, but there is enough information for us to get a general idea of what to expect.

The long, dark shadow of biblical prophecies about the Antichrist fall across the pages of human history. They remind us that one day there will come a world leader of such irresistible magnitude that the world will be swept off its feet. He will charm the public, deceive the nations, and control the planet.

Since Satan himself does not know the exact time of Christ's return, he must have a potential candidate for the Antichrist ready at all times. How can we know who he is? What will happen when he rises to power? When will he come on the scene? The biblical record provides us with numerous clues to the identity of the Antichrist. My purpose is to examine those clues and shed light on the identity of this shadowy figure who is destined to control the world through the social, political, and religious structures of the last days.

There are more than 100 passages of Scripture that describe the Antichrist's origin, nationality, character, career, and global conquest. My goal is to explain, define, and refine the prophetic materials about the Antichrist. I have gone out of the way to avoid ridiculous and unnecessary speculation.

The term *Antichrist* may be applied both to an individual and the system he represents. Since he will control these structures to his advantage, it is also vital that we renew our commitment to serve the cause of Christ in this world until the Savior calls us home. We have no mandate to surrender this world to Satan. On the contrary, we are called to transform society by the power of the gospel until our work here is done.

Someone ominous is looming on the horizon of human existence. He may still be in the shadows for the moment, but he could suddenly burst forth on the world scene at any time. In the meantime, let us proclaim the truth of the One who is the Light of the world. Keep looking up!

—Ed Hindson
There's Hope! Ministries
Atlanta, GA

The Coming World Ruler

*Who is like the beast? Who can make
war against him?*

—Revelation 13:4

Biblical prophecies clearly predict the rise of the Antichrist in the end times. Many people believe the great millennial end-game has already begun. As civilization speeds toward its final destiny, the appearance of a powerful world ruler is inevitable. The ultimate question facing our generation is whether he is already alive and well and moving into power. This book is an attempt to answer the questions most frequently asked about the Antichrist. How can we know who he is? What clues are there to his identity? When will he make his move to control the global economy and world politics?

The Bible predicts that worldwide chaos, instability, and disorder will increase as we approach the end of the age. Jesus predicted there would be "wars and rumors of wars . . . [and] famines and earthquakes in various places" (Matthew 24:6,7). Dr. Ed Dobson observes, "The Bible also predicts that this chaos will pave the way for the rise of a new world leader who will be able to negotiate world peace and deliver on the promise of security and harmony. This world leader is a person whom most Bible students call the Antichrist."[1]

Ironically, the term *Antichrist* appears only in 1 John 2:18-22 and 4:3. The apostle John uses it both in the singular ("the antichrist") and in the plural ("many antichrists"). John indicates that his readers have already heard that *the* Antichrist is coming in the future. Then he surprises them by announcing that *many* antichrists have already come. He defines these lesser antichrists as liars who deny that Jesus is the Christ (2:22). In this sense, an antichrist is any false teacher who denies the person and work of Jesus Christ. Such teachers are truly *anti* ("against") Christ.

In 1 John 4:1-3, John warns us to test the spirits to make sure they are from God. Again, he warns that many false prophets (Greek, *pseudoprophetes*) are "gone out into the world." These are the people who don't acknowledge that Jesus is from God. In this sense, John announces that the "spirit of the antichrist . . . is already in the world."

Spirit of the Antichrist

In the broadest use of the concept of the "spirit of the Antichrist," we can say with certainty that it is already at work. It is this anti-Christian spirit that does everything it can to undermine, deny, and reject the truth about Jesus Christ. That spirit has been here since the first century, actively opposing the work of Christ on earth.

Dr. Gregory Boyd points out that spiritual conflict is the reality of our universe. In his powerful book *God at War,* Boyd writes, "One is hard pressed to find any culture, prior to or contemporary with our own, that does not assume something like this perspective. . . . From a cross-cultural perspective, the insight that the cosmos is teeming with spiritual beings . . . is simply common sense. It is we modern Westerners who are the oddballs for thinking that we are the only agents who influence other people."[2]

There can be no doubt that the biblical writers believed the spirit of the Antichrist was alive and well in the first century A.D. Therefore, they were not surprised by opposition, persecution, and even martyrdom. They were convinced that the spiritual war between Christ and Antichrist had already begun.

Grant Jeffrey provides numerous examples of early Christian references to the Antichrist in the *Apocalypse of Peter,* the *Didache,* the *Ascension of Isaiah,* and the *Pseudo-Titus Epistle,* as well as various church fathers such as Irenaeus, Jerome, and Hippolytus.[3] Irenaeus, who studied under Polycarp, who in turn was discipled by the apostle John, said the Antichrist shall come as "an apostate," the very embodiment of "satanic apostasy."[4]

From the very beginning of the Christian era, believers were convinced that a world ruler would eventually come on the scene who was the embodiment of Satan. The book of Revelation (chapters 12–13) presents an "unholy trinity" that aligns Satan (vs. Father), Antichrist (vs. Son), and False Prophet (vs. Holy Spirit). Thus, the real power behind the Antichrist is Satan. The "father of lies" is the perpetrator of the human manifestation of the world's greatest liar and the source of the lie that will condemn multitudes under divine judgment (2 Thessalonians 2:11).

Titles of the Antichrist

The person we commonly refer to as the Antichrist is actually known by several names and titles throughout the Bible. Each of these provides a glimpse of the many facets of his diabolical character and nature and presents a portrait of the Antichrist in a series of word pictures that leave little to the imagination.

The Beast

"I saw a beast coming out of the sea. He had ten horns and seven heads, with ten crowns on his horns, and on each head a blasphemous name" (Revelation 13:1).

The Man of Destruction

"Don't let anyone deceive you in any way, for that day will not come until the rebellion occurs and the man of lawlessness is revealed, the man doomed to destruction" (2 Thessalonians 2:3).

The Lawless One

"And then the lawless one will be revealed, whom the Lord Jesus will overthrow with the breath of his mouth and destroy by the splendor of his coming" (2 Thessalonians 2:8).

The Abomination

"So when you see standing in the holy place 'the abomination that causes desolation,' spoken of through the prophet Daniel . . ." (Matthew 24:15).

The Little Horn

"While I was thinking about the horns, there before me was another horn, a little one, which came up among them; and three of the first horns were uprooted before it. This horn had eyes like the eyes of a man and a mouth that spoke boastfully" (Daniel 7:8).

The Insolent King

"In the latter part of their reign, when rebels have become completely wicked, a stern-faced king, a master of intrigue, will arise" (Daniel 8:23).

The Ruler Who Is to Come

"After the sixty-two 'sevens,' the Anointed One will be cut off and will have nothing. The people of the ruler who will come will destroy the city and the sanctuary" (Daniel 9:26).

The Despicable Person

"He will be succeeded by a contemptible person who has not been given the honor of royalty. He will invade the kingdom when its people feel secure, and he will seize it through intrigue" (Daniel 11:21).

The Strong-Willed King

"The king will do as he pleases. He will exalt and magnify himself above every god and will say unheard-of things against the God of gods. He will be successful until the time of wrath is completed, for what has been determined must take place" (Daniel 11:36).

The Worthless Shepherd

"For I am going to raise up a shepherd over the land who will not care for the lost, or seek the young, or heal the injured, or feed the healthy, but will eat the meat of the choice sheep, tearing off their hoofs. Woe to the worthless shepherd, who deserts the flock!" (Zechariah 11:16,17).

The Antichrist

"Dear children, this is the last hour; and as you have heard that the antichrist is coming, even now many antichrists have come. . . . Who is the liar? It is the man who denies that Jesus is the Christ. Such a man is the antichrist" (1 John 2:18,22).

A great deal has been written about the prefix *anti* in connection with the Antichrist. It can mean either "against" (in opposition to) or "instead of" (in place of). The issue comes down to whether he is the great enemy of Christ or whether he is a false Christ. If he is the enemy of Christ and the head of a Gentile world government, then he is most likely to be a Gentile himself. If he is a false messiah who is accepted by the Jews, then it would stand to reason that he would be Jewish.

Richard Trench writes, "The distinction, then, is plain . . . *antichristos* (antichrist) denies that there is a Christ; *pseudochristos* (false Christ) affirms himself to be Christ."[5] The biblical picture is that he is *both*. Initially, he presents himself as the "savior" of Israel by making a covenant to protect her (Daniel 9:27). In this manner, he appears to be her long-awaited Messiah. But in reality, he is against all that the messianic prophecies foretell about the true Messiah.

His Nationality

Whether the Antichrist is a Jew or a Gentile is not clearly answered in the New Testament. Most prophetic scholars believe he will be a Gentile because:

1. he leads the European Union of Gentile nations (Daniel 7:8-24).

2. his covenant with Israel promises Gentile protection for Israel (Daniel 9:27).

3. his rule is part of the "times of the Gentiles" and their domination over Israel (Luke 21:24).

These passages make it clear that the Antichrist will lead the Western powers, but they do not specifically designate him as a Gentile. It is entirely possible that he could be of Jewish origin or nationality and still be a European or American Jew who leads the final form of the world government. The fact that the verse that says he will not regard the "God of his fathers" (KJV) can also be translated "gods of his fathers" (NIV). This makes his background inconclusive. However the typical exegesis of Daniel 11:37 has focused on his atheistic beliefs, regardless of whether he is a Jew or Gentile.[6]

Stephen Miller writes, "This verse states that Antichrist will reject whatever religion is practiced by his ancestors."[7] Charles Feinberg, on the other hand, prefers the reading "God of his fathers" (KJV), noting that this is the usual expression in the Old Testament for the "God of Abraham, Isaac and Jacob." Feinberg adds, "This is the name of God that is used in the prayer book of the Jews to this very day."[8] Either way, the Antichrist is clearly said to be an unbeliever.

Both the books of Daniel and Revelation associate the Antichrist with a confederation of ten European nations that correspond in some way to the old Roman Empire. Daniel 2:31-45 symbolizes this by the ten *toes* of the great statue in Nebuchadnezzar's dream. Daniel 7:19-28 and Revelation 13:1-9 symbolize this by the ten *horns* on the beast.

In Daniel's prophecies, the Antichrist is always associated with the final phase of the Roman Empire (fourth kingdom). In Revelation 17:9, he is identified with a city that sits on "seven hills" (Rome). While John uses the symbolic term *Mystery Babylon* to describe this city, he clearly indicates that he is talking about Rome.

Arno Froese points out that the entire social-political-legal structure of the Western world is essentially European. He writes, "The populations of the USA, Canada and South America are made up mainly of European descendents. Our governments are based on Roman principles. . . . We do well to remember that America, North and South, most of Africa, and Australia are a political reality due to . . . the greatest power structure ever, Europe."[9]

It is not difficult, given our current international structure and the need for a human leader to guarantee peaceful coexistence, to imagine a powerful world ruler coming on the scene in the immediate future. The same spirit of Antichrist is at work today, attempting to lure this world into the lap of Satan. Harvard theologian Harvey Cox has warned, "The greatest seducers of history all had one thing in common: they could use the natural needs and instincts of another person for their own selfish ends." He argued that seduction is the most callous form of exploitation because "it tricks the victim into becoming an unwitting accomplice in his own seduction."[10]

His Genius and Power

The Antichrist will be the most incredible leader the world has ever known. On the surface he will appear to be the epitome of human genius and power. Arthur W. Pink writes, "Satan has had full opportunity afforded him to study fallen human nature. . . . The devil knows full well how to dazzle people by the attraction of power. . . . He knows how to gratify the craving for knowledge. . . . He can delight the ear with music and the eye with entrancing beauty. . . . He knows how to exalt people to dizzy heights of worldly greatness and fame, and how to control that greatness so that it may be employed against God and His people."[11]

Pink provides the following list of the characteristics of the Antichrist:

1. Intellectual genius (Daniel 7:20).

2. Oratorical genius (Daniel 7:20).

3. Political genius (Daniel 11:21).

4. Commercial genius (Daniel 8:25).

5. Military genius (Daniel 8:24).

6. Administrative genius (Revelation 13:1-2).

7. Religious genius (2 Thessalonians 2:4).

Perhaps the most telling of his characteristics is depicted in Daniel 11:21, which tells us that he will come to power and "seize it through intrigue" ("flatteries," KJV). Here is a *master of deception*, empowered by the "father of lies." Many believe he will be Satan incarnate—thus his miraculous recovery in Revelation 13:3.

Grant Jeffrey points out several contrasts between Christ and Antichrist.[12] These include:

Christ	Antichrist
The Truth	The Lie
Holy One	Lawless One
Man of Sorrows	Man of Sin
Son of God	Son of Satan
Mystery of Godliness	Mystery of Iniquity
Good Shepherd	Worthless Shepherd
Exalted on High	Cast Down to Hell
Humbled Himself	Exalted Himself
Despised	Admired
Cleanses the Temple	Defiles the Temple
Slain for the People	Slays the People
The Lamb	The Beast

A simple survey of the characteristics of the Antichrist confirms the idea that he is both a false Christ (*pseudochristos*) and against Christ (*antichristos*). He masquerades as an angel of light only to plunge the world into spiritual darkness. Like Satan, he is a destroyer, not a builder. Promising peace, he pushes the world into war. In every conceivable way, he is just like Satan who indwells and empowers him.

Is He Alive Today?

The spirit of Antichrist is alive and well! It is the Satan-inspired expression of lawlessness and rebellion against God, the things of God, and the people of God. It has been alive since Satan slithered his way around the Garden of

Eden. It has been the driving force behind the whole terrible history of the human race—wars, murders, thefts, and rapes. It is the ugly expression of the destructive nature of the great deceiver himself.

The New Testament authors assure us that the spirit of Antichrist was active in their day over 20 centuries ago. It has remained active throughout the whole of church history, expressing itself in persecutions, heresies, spiritual deceptions, false prophets, and false religions. Satan has battled the church at every turn throughout its long history, waiting for the right moment to indwell the right person—the Antichrist—as his final masterpiece.

Guessing whether certain contemporary figures might be the Antichrist, however, has always proven futile. Viewing the future through the eyes of the present led to some fantastic speculations in the twentieth century alone. Here is just a sampling of the proposals that have been offered:

Kaiser Wilhelm

The German emperor's title meant "Caesar," and he intended to conquer all of Europe in World War I and reunite the old Roman Empire.

Benito Mussolini

The Italian strongman from Rome threatened the world after World War I, and prophetic speculators tagged him as the Antichrist long before World War II began.

Adolph Hitler

Hitler has come to represent the ultimate personification of evil. He persecuted and murdered 15 million people (6 million were Jews) and tried to conquer all of Europe but failed.

Joseph Stalin

This atheistic leader of the former Soviet Union was known for his political intrigues, brutal assassinations, and desire to conquer the world under the banner of communism.

Nikita Krushchev

Many people still remember the leader of the former Soviet Union pounding his shoe on the podium of the United Nations and threatening to bury us all.

John F. Kennedy

Anti-Catholic fundamentalists were convinced that Kennedy was going to form an alliance with the pope and the communists and take over the world.

Mikhail Gorbachev

Many believed he was only deceiving the West into reducing its nuclear arsenal. Some even suggested a red mark on his head might be the "mark of the beast."

Ronald Wilson Reagan

Yes, even the darling of politically conservative Evangelicals was targeted as a candidate for the Antichrist because he had six letters in each of his three names (666).

Saddam Hussein

Some have suggested that he will sign a peace treaty with Israel only to break it and renew his hostilities toward the Promised Land.

Bill Clinton

Some believe Bill Clinton is the Antichrist and Hillary is the False Prophet.

Other candidates for Antichrist have included Henry Kissinger, Margaret Thatcher, Boris Yeltsin, and George Bush. The problem with these identifications is they are always tentative and viewed through the cultural lens of our own times. The real tragedy is that people guessing dates and selecting possibilities for the Antichrist are claiming to know more than the writers of Scripture. Jesus Himself said, "No one knows about that day or hour, not even the angels in heaven, nor the Son, but only the Father" (Matthew 24:36). Someone will inevitably point out that this says the "day" or "hour," and not the "year." But the obvious point of this passage is that no one knows the time, so don't waste your time trying to guess the time. Be ready all the time because Jesus could come at any time!

The Restless Search

Any apparent delay is not due to God's indecision, but to the fact that He has not let us in on the secret. Nor has He revealed this to Satan, who is a limited, finite being. Satan himself is left guessing when the rapture might occur. This means he must have a man in mind to indwell as the Antichrist in every generation. In other words, any one of a number of people could have been the Antichrist, but only one will be. Satan too must keep selecting candidates and waiting for God's timing.

The apostle Paul comments on this in 2 Thessalonians 2:1-12, when he tells us that the "coming of our Lord Jesus" will not happen until the "rebellion occurs" and the "man of lawlessness is revealed" (verse 3). Next, he tells us that "you know what is holding him back, so that he may be revealed at the proper time" (verse 6). Only after the rapture of the church will the identity of the Antichrist be revealed. In other words, you don't want to know who he is. If you ever do figure out who he is, you have been left behind!

Since Satan must prepare a man to be his crowning achievement in every generation, it should not surprise us that several candidates appear on the horizon of human history only to vanish away. Satan must wait on God's timing, so he is defeated before he ever begins his final assault on God. He can't make his move until God releases the restraining power of the Holy Spirit indwelling the church. Therefore, the Spirit is the agent and the church is the means by which God restrains Satan's diabolical plan until the Father calls us home to heaven.

Satan's doom is already assured, but the battle is far from being over. He still "prowls around like a roaring lion looking for someone to devour" (1 Peter 5:8). He has fallen from heaven (Isaiah 14:12). He was condemned in Eden (Genesis 3:14). He accuses the believers (Revelation 12:10). Eventually he will be cast out of heaven permanently and will expend his wrath on the earth (Revelation 12:7-12). Ultimately he will be defeated at Armageddon and cast into the abyss (Revelation 19:11–20:3). Finally he will be thrown into the lake of fire (Revelation 20:10).

In the meantime, Satan waits for his opportunity to destroy the whole world and the ultimate plan of God. He may be a defeated foe, but he has every intention of keeping up the fight to the very end. Even now he is moving about restlessly, searching for the right man to be the Antichrist.

Ten Keys to His Identity

The Bible gives us at least ten keys to identifying the Antichrist when he does come to power. They provide enough details to give a general idea of who he will be when Satan inspires him to make his move onto the world scene. These clues also make it clear that only one person in history will fit this description. There have been many prototypes, but there will only be one Antichrist.

1. *He will rise to power in the last days:* "Later in the time of wrath [the time of the end] . . . a stern-faced king, a master of intrigue, will arise" (Daniel 8:19,23).

2. *He will rule the whole world:* "And he was given authority over every tribe, people, language and nation" (Revelation 13:7).

3. *His headquarters will be in Rome:* "The beast, which you saw, once was, now is not, and will come up out of the Abyss. . . . The seven heads are seven hills on which the woman sits" (Revelation 17:8,9).

4. *He is intelligent and persuasive:* "The other horn . . . looked more imposing than the others and . . . had eyes and a mouth that spoke boastfully" (Daniel 7:20).

5. *He rules by international consent:* "The ten horns you saw are ten kings. . . . They have one purpose and will give their power and authority to the beast" (Revelation 17:12,13).

6. *He rules by deception:* "He will become very strong . . . and will succeed in whatever he does. . . .

He will cause deceit to prosper, and he will consider himself superior" (Daniel 8:24,25).

7. *He controls the global economy:* "He also forced everyone, small and great, rich and poor, free and slave, to receive a mark on his right hand or on his forehead, so that no one could buy or sell unless he had the mark, which is the name of the beast or the number of his name" (Revelation 13:16,17).

8. *He will make a peace treaty with Israel:* "He will confirm a covenant with many for one 'seven.' In the middle of that 'seven' he will put an end to sacrifice and offering" (Daniel 9:27).

9. *He will break the treaty and invade Israel:* "The people of the ruler who will come will destroy the city and the sanctuary. The end will come like a flood: War will continue until the end, and desolations have been decreed" (Daniel 9:26).

10. *He will claim to be God:* "He will oppose and will exalt himself over everything that is called God or is worshiped, so that he sets himself up in God's temple, proclaiming himself to be God" (2 Thessalonians 2:4).

There are many other details given in the Bible regarding the person we commonly call the Antichrist. But the general picture is that of a European (American?) who rises to power over the Western world. Whether he is Jewish or Gentile is not entirely clear. What is clear, however, is that he will control the last great bastion of Gentile world power. From his base in the West, he will extend his control over the entire world. For all practical purposes, he will administrate the world government and the global economy, assisted by the leader of the world religion (Revelation 13:11-18). He may be moving into power at this very moment. Only time will reveal his true identity.

When he does come to power, the Antichrist will apparently be promising to ensure world peace through a series of international alliances, treaties, and agreements (see Daniel 8:24; Revelation 17:12). Despite his promises of peace, his international policies will inevitably plunge the world into the greatest war of all time.

2

The Ultimate Deception

Then I saw another beast. . . . He
deceived the inhabitants of the earth.
—Revelation 13:11,14

The Antichrist will not rise to power alone. His success will result from a worldwide spiritual deception perpetrated by the False Prophet. His ability to perform miraculous signs will enable him to convince the public that the Antichrist is the leader for whom they have been looking. The ultimate deception of the end times will involve the worldwide worship of the Antichrist. This will be encouraged by the False Prophet (Revelation 19:20; 20:10), also known as the second "beast" (Revelation 13:11-17). Like the Antichrist, his identity is not clearly revealed, but several clues are given to help us know who he is.

J. Dwight Pentecost observes that the False Prophet serves as the spokesperson for the Antichrist. He states that the spirit of Antichrist "will culminate in the Beasts in their corporate ministries. . . . The first Beast will be in direct opposition to Christ . . . and the second Beast will assume the place of leadership in the religious realm which rightly belongs to Christ."[1]

Revelation 13 presents ten identifying features of the False Prophet:

1. rises out of the earth (13:11)

2. controls religious affairs (13:11)

3. motivated by Satan (13:11)

4. promotes the worship of the beast (13:12)

5. performs signs and miracles (13:13)

6. deceives the whole world (13:14)

7. empowers the image of the beast (13:15)

8. kills all who refuse to worship (13:15)

9. controls all economic commerce (13:17)

10. controls the mark of the beast (13:17,18)

Biblical scholars are divided on the matter of the identity of the False Prophet. Some believe that he will be Jewish, while others believe he will be a Gentile. The biblical record itself is inconclusive. However, when we observe the relationship of the False Prophet to the great prostitute (Revelation 17), we immediately notice his connection to the city on "seven hills" (see 17:7,9) that rules "over the kings of the earth" (17–18). It seems clear that

John is referring to Rome by the terminology that he uses to describe the symbol of "Babylon the Great."

Ironically, little has been written about the False Prophet compared to the volumes of material about the Antichrist.[2] Thomas Ice and Timothy Demy comment, "The Antichrist and the False Prophet are two separate individuals who will work toward a common, deceptive goal. Their roles and relationship will be that which was common in the ancient world between a ruler (Antichrist) and the high priest (False Prophet) of the national religion.[3]

Work of the False Prophet

The False Prophet is depicted in the Revelation as one who uses miraculous signs and wonders to deceive the world into worshiping the Antichrist. Ice and Demy remark, "Even though this is yet a future event, the lesson to be learned for our own day is that one must exercise discernment, especially in the area of religion—even when miracles appear to vindicate the messenger."[4]

A century ago, Samuel Andrews argued that the work of the False Prophet will be to extend his ecclesiastical administration over the whole earth by establishing the church of the Antichrist as the counterfeit of the true church.[5] Andrews viewed this apostate religion as being bound together by a common hatred of Christianity and being filled with demonical power. Thus, the False Prophet does not so much deny Christian doctrine as he corrupts it. Only in this way can the Antichrist sit in the temple of God, demanding to be worshiped as God (see Isaiah 14:12-14). Remember, in Satan's temptation of Christ, he also appealed for worship (Matthew 4:8-10). In fact, Satan offered to surrender the entire world to Christ if He would worship him. Therefore, it should not surprise us that the goal of the Satan-inspired False Prophet will be to get the whole world to bow down to the Antichrist, who is the personification of Satan himself.

Together, Satan (dragon), Antichrist (beast of sea), and the False Prophet (beast of earth) comprise an "unholy trinity" that is a counterfeit of the triune God. Satan opposes the Father; Antichrist opposes the Son; and the False Prophet opposes the Holy Spirit. This ungodly alliance is Satan's final attempt to overthrow the work of God on earth.

The method of their diabolical attempt is explained in the biblical record. The Antichrist dare not appear until after the "rebellion" (NIV) or "falling away" (KJV) of apostasy. In the meantime, the spirit of Antichrist (lawlessness) is already at work attempting to pervert the gospel and to corrupt the true church. When this process is sufficiently established, the False Prophet will arise to prepare for the coming of the Antichrist.

Spiritual Prostitution

The False Prophet is identified in Revelation 17 with the "great prostitute" (apostate religion). Dr. John Walvoord observes, "Prostitution was often a part of pagan worship, but the adultery mentioned here refers to spiritual adultery. The woman is guilty of compromise and association with apostate religions."[6]

Walter K. Price draws numerous parallels between the Antichrist and Antiochus IV Epiphanes, who persecuted the Jews in the second century B.C. He writes, "The false prophet is to the Antichrist what Menelaus was to Antiochus IV.

Menelaus was responsible for enforcing many of the Hellenizing decrees of Antiochus IV upon his own people, the Jews."[7]

The False Prophet is depicted as having "two horns like a lamb, but he spoke like a dragon" (Revelation 13:11). He looks religious, but he talks like the devil. He counterfeits true religion in order to hide his real identity. Price states, "Just as the Holy Spirit is dedicated to bringing the world to know Jesus Christ, the False Prophet is dedicated to bringing all men into spiritual allegiance with the Antichrist."[8]

The process by which the False Prophet deceives the world is through apostasy, the renunciation of the true gospel. The spirit of Antichrist continues to work throughout church history, daring to deny the true Savior and His work on the cross that redeemed us from our sins.

Religious Apostasy

Puritan scholar John Owen observed that apostasy is brought about by the great apostate himself. He wrote, "The devil, that greatest of all apostates, has it as his chief desire to destroy Christ's church on earth, and failing that, to utterly corrupt it and so make it his church."[9]

Owen pictures Satan's external attacks against the church as a roaring lion and his internal attacks as a poisonous serpent. It is the latter that has proven most insidious. Owen adds, "Once in, he secretly and gradually poisoned the minds of many by vain thought of power and ambition, with love for the praise and honor of the world, and with superstitions. Thus he turned them from the spiritual power and simplicity of the gospel. . . . In this way, the 'mystery of iniquity' worked and was successful."[10]

Owen goes on to list the danger signs of *apostasy:*[11]

1. loss of all appreciation for the gospel

2. loss of conviction that the gospel is true

3. contempt for the promises of God

4. rejection of the true Christian religion

5. despises and rejects people of God

6. despises and rejects the Spirit of God

7. open declaration of hatred for Christ

Though these observations were made over 300 years ago, they pinpoint exactly the nature of apostasy, both personal and ecclesiastical. When professing Christians turn against the truth, they often do so with a vengeance. Anyone who has ever debated theological issues with extreme liberals has felt their bitterness and enmity against the Savior.

It should not surprise us then that the False Prophet represents the apostate religion of the end times. If his rise to power parallels that of the Antichrist, he will preside over apostate Christendom after the rapture of true believers to heaven. All that are left behind—be they Catholic, Protestant, Evangelical, or Charismatic—will be lost. In such an environment, the False Prophet will have no problem deceiving the whole world. While the Holy Spirit will still be omnipresent in the world, the removal of the church (body of Christ) will bring His restraining ministry to an end.

The Great Lie

The apostle Paul explained this process when he wrote: "For the secret power of lawlessness is already at work; but the one who now holds it back will continue to do so till he is taken out of the way" (2 Thessalonians 2:7). After the rapture, the Holy Spirit will still convict people of sin, but His restraining ministry will be over and all of Satan's evil will break loose on earth. Then the lawless one will be revealed. Paul said, "The coming of the lawless one will be in accordance with the work of Satan displayed in all kinds of counterfeit miracles, signs and wonders, and in every sort of evil that deceives those who are perishing" (2 Thessalonians 2:9,10). The rise of the Antichrist ("lawless one") will parallel a general breakdown in religious and moral values, resulting in a decadent society that will believe "the lie" rather than the truth.

The apostle does not define "the lie" (Greek, *psuedei*), but he specifies that it is a particular lie, not just any lie. It is possible that this could refer to a falsehood perpetrated to explain away the rapture (for example, alien abductions). But it is more likely that it is the official rejection of Christ and the acceptance of the deification and worship of the Antichrist.

The False Prophet is presented in the Revelation as an individual who is empowered by Satan (13:11,12). Later, he is personally cast into the lake of fire (19:20; 20:10). However, the religious system that he represents is called the "great prostitute" (17:1) who is drunk with the "blood of the saints" (17:6). Therefore, the final phase of apostasy is both a religious system and the individual who leads it. Herman Hoyt observes, "The harlot, representing all false religion at last united in one great super-organization, will ride the beast."[12]

The Final Religion

A great deal has been written about the false religion of the last days. Several identifications have been suggested. Medieval Catholic scholars pointed to Mohammed as the False Prophet. Protestant reformers were convinced it was the pope. More recent identifications have included the National Council of Churches, the New Age movement, and various religious cults.

A few observations are in order here. First, the apostles were convinced that the spirit of Antichrist (1 John 4:3) and the mystery of iniquity (2 Thessalonians 2:7, KJV) were already at work in their own time. This means that the apostate spirit predates all modern churches as we know them today. Second, the final, future form of apostasy is clearly located in the city of the Antichrist at Rome (Revelation 17:9), referred to symbolically as "Babylon the Great" (Revelation 18:2).

If pretribulationists are correct in assuming the rapture of the true church will occur before the tribulation period, then all "Christian" churches that remain will be apostate, no matter what their label—Catholic, Reformed, Methodist, Baptist, or Pentecostal. It is a very reasonable assumption that all those "pseudo-Christians" left behind would align with one another in a common cause of unbelief (2 Thessalonians 2:8-12). It is also reasonable to assume that whoever serves as pope at that time will be an unbeliever and use his position and authority to encourage such an alliance of unbelieving Christendom. The ecclesiastical unity liberal Christendom has so long failed to produce will occur instantly after the rapture.

Consider these important observations:

1. The spirit of Antichrist and the mystery of iniquity were *already at work* in apostolic times.

2. Apostasy has *progressed throughout church history*, predating modern church structures.

3. A large segment of modern Christendom is *already apostate*. Unbelief is rampant in both liberal Catholic and Protestant circles.

4. *After the rapture* of true believers, all professing "Christians" who are left behind will be apostate believers no matter what their denomination.

5. The False Prophet will arise in Rome to lead *apostate Christendom* in its acceptance of the Antichrist.

The Enemy Within

The New Testament was written in the first century A.D. when Roman paganism and emperor worship threatened the church. Despite this external threat, the biblical writers warned constantly of apostasy from within the ranks of the church (see 1 Timothy 4:1-3; 2 Timothy 3:1-5; 2 Corinthians 11:13-15; Galatians 1:6-12; 2 Peter 2:1-3; 1 John 4:1-3; 2 John 7; Jude 3,4). In 2 Thessalonians 2:3-12, Paul describes this *apostasy* in the following terms:

1. the rebellion (verse 3)

2. secret power of lawlessness (verse 7)

3. the work of Satan (verse 9)

4. powerful delusion (verse 11)

5. the lie (verse 11)

Paul indicates that this process will begin during the Church Age. The "falling away" (KJV; Greek, *apostasia*) will occur before the "coming of our Lord Jesus Christ" (2:1,3). But its final explosion as a form of worldwide unbelief will only occur after the restraining ministry of the Holy Spirit indwelling the true church is removed at the rapture (2:5-8).

This seems to clearly indicate that we will probably not know who the False Prophet is prior to the rapture. But we can certainly observe several *characteristics of the apostasy* as we near the end of the age. The biblical writers use the following descriptions:

1. abandon the faith (1 Timothy 4:1)

2. follow deceiving spirits (1 Timothy 4:1)

3. doctrines of demons (1 Timothy 4:1)

4. hypocritical liars (1 Timothy 4:2)

5. lovers of themselves (2 Timothy 3:2)

6. lovers of money (2 Timothy 3:2)

7. boastful, proud, abusive, unholy (2 Timothy 3:2)

8. lovers of pleasure (2 Timothy 3:4)

9. deceitful workmen (2 Corinthians 11:13)

10. pervert the gospel of Christ (Galatians 1:7)

11. destructive heresies (2 Peter 2:1)

12. shameful ways (2 Peter 2:2)

13. deceivers (2 John 7)

14. godless men (Jude 4)

15. Christ-deniers (Jude 4)

The New Testament also provides a list of categorical descriptions for these apostates. In most cases the Greek term *pseudo* ("false") is prefixed to a legitimate category, implying that apostates are false imitators of the real thing. They are called:

1. false christs, *pseudochristoi* (Matthew 24:24)

2. false prophets, *pseudoprophetai* (Matthew 24:11)

3. false apostles, *pseudoapostoloi* (2 Corinthians 11:13)

4. false teachers, *pseudodidaskaloi* (2 Peter 2:1)

5. false brothers, *pseudoadelphoi* (Galatians 2:4)

These designations imply that an apostate form of Christendom will be the final world religion of the last days. Whether this religion will include unbelieving elements of other religious faiths only time will tell. The final world religion could be amalgamated from a general religious tolerance, a perversion of Christianity, or a subjective religious climate in which each person does his or her own thing while generally acknowledging the worship of the Antichrist as God.

The Bible clearly predicts *three major institutions* at the time of the end:

1. world government

2. global economy

3. world religion

The first two are already in place. The world government functions through the United Nations, backed by American and European firepower. The global economy is a reality. You can purchase anything in the world with a credit card almost instantly. The world religion will be a tougher sell, but a dramatic global event—like the rapture—would accelerate worldwide religious cooperation in a matter of weeks.

Image of the Beast

Part of the deception perpetrated by the False Prophet will be his power to give life to the "image of the beast" (Revelation 13:15). The biblical text uses the word *eikon* ("icon") for "image." It means a representation derived from a prototype or a "perfect likeness." It looks like the real thing, but it isn't. While we cannot be certain what "image of the beast" refers to, more and more scholars are suggesting the possibility of a televised holographic image or a computer icon.

Television is *the* national pastime in America. We spend more time watching it than any other activity except sleeping. It has changed our ideas about marriage, family life, personal morality, and even politics. Television, more than any other aspect of our culture, sets the agenda for our society. It tells us what is important and meaningful in our lives. In many cases, it even determines when we get up and when we go to bed.

In their national bestseller, *Remote Control: Television and the Manipulation of American Life*, Frank Mankiewicz and Joel Swerdlow state, "Television is more powerful than any other institution in America today."[13] They note: "A bestselling book may reach several million people . . . a hit movie is seen by perhaps 6 million people . . . the nation's largest-circulation newspaper has 2 million readers. But a television program which enters less than 30 million homes is a failure."[14]

Ninety-seven percent of all American households have at least one television set, outnumbering homes that are equipped with refrigerators or indoor toilets. The average American watches nearly four hours of television per day, meaning that he or she will spend nine years of life in front of a television set. By the time a youngster reaches the age of 15, he or she will witness 12,000 acts of violence. The authors of *Remote Control* observe, "If one wishes to see fifty-four acts of violence, one can watch all the plays of Shakespeare, or one can watch three evenings (sometimes only two) of prime-time television."[15]

Most of us who were raised on television from our earliest childhood do not think in the same patterns as did our parents and grandparents before us. According to one study, "The Television Generation consists roughly of all people born since 1945."[16] It is this generation that urged that one school give Captain Kangaroo an honorary doctorate and that the actor who played television doctor Marcus Welby be invited to speak at a medical school commencement!

Alistair Cooke observed, "Television has produced a generation of children who have a declining grasp of the English language, but have a visual sophistication that was denied to their parents."[17] Unfortunately, he warns, the power of television images appeals more to the emotions than the intellect and bypasses critical aspects of judgment.

In 1938, author E.B. White predicted that television would become the test of the modern world. "We shall stand or fall by television," he warned.[18] While observing that television would expand our visual perception of reality, he also cautioned that the televised images would appear so real that, in time, we would no longer see the difference between the real and the unreal. Even the pain in

another's face would leave "the impression of mere arti-
fice."[19]

The power of televised images is so incredible, and yet
so subtle, that most of us do not yet comprehend what they
mean to our society. Harvey Cox has observed that the
"new media, especially those dealing in pictorial images,
are immensely powerful. . . . TV reaches us at a level of consciousness below the critically centered intelligence."[20] He
went on to observe that broadcast technology tends to
make us all "quiescent consumers" victimized by the power
of transmission. "Programs create, and then suggest ways to
satisfy human needs," he stated. "But the process is one of
seduction."[21]

One of the great dangers of television is that it sends a
message to the viewer that tells him he is getting what he
wants and needs. Instead of meeting the viewer's real needs,
mass media actually determine what those needs will be.
Thus, it is no wonder that biblical prophecy speaks of the
Antichrist in terms of the "image of the beast" (Revelation
13:15).

Spiritual deception is the goal of the False Prophet as he
encourages people to embrace the social, economic, and
religious program of the Antichrist. These sweeping
changes will occur more rapidly using the power of television and the wide-spread access to information through
computer technology. As we approach the end of the age,
false prophets, new religions, and spiritual darkness will
engulf the world.

Rise of False Prophets

---

*Watch out that no one deceives
you. . . . False prophets will appear
and deceive many* people.

—Matthew 24:4,11

Spiritual deception by false prophets is not a new phenomenon. False prophecies have been around as long as
there have been legitimate prophets of God. Moses raised
the question to the children of Israel: "How can we know
when a message has not been spoken by the LORD?" His
answer was, "If what a prophet proclaims in the name of
the LORD does not take place or come true, that is a message
the LORD has not spoken. That prophet has spoken pre-
sumptuously. Do not be afraid of him" (Deuteronomy
18:21,22). A true prophet—

1. must speak in the name of the Lord, not some other god.

2. must have a message that is in accord with God's revealed truth in Scripture.

3. must give predictions of future events that come true *exactly* as stated.

One of the most scathing denunciations of false prophets in all of Scripture is delivered by the prophet Jeremiah. In his time, Jeremiah had to deal constantly with false prophets who opposed his ministry, contradicted his message, and even conspired to have him killed. They kept telling the leaders of Jerusalem that the people had nothing to fear from the Babylonian invaders, but Jeremiah knew differently. Jerusalem was on the verge of destruction, and the people were about to be taken into captivity for 70 years.

"My heart is broken within me," Jeremiah confesses in his agony over these false prophets who ". . . follow an evil course and use their power unjustly" (Jeremiah 23:9,10). "Both prophet and priest are godless," the Lord responds (23:11). Then He tells Jeremiah His opinion of these false prophets:

> Do not listen to what the prophets are prophesying to you; they fill you with false hopes. They speak visions from their own minds, not from the mouth of the LORD (verse 16).

> I did not send these prophets, yet they have run with their message; I did not speak to them, yet they have prophesied (verse 21).

> I have heard what the prophets say who prophesy lies in my name. They say, "I had a dream! I had a

dream!" How long will this continue in the hearts of these lying prophets, who prophesy the delusions of their own minds? (verse 25)

Yes . . . I am against the prophets who wag their own tongues. . . . Indeed, I am against those who prophesy false dreams. . . . Because every man's own word becomes his oracle and so you distort the words of the living God, the LORD Almighty, our God (verses 31,32,36).

Jeremiah could not make his complaint any clearer or his case any stronger. God is against those false prophets whose spiritual delusion causes them to invent their own message apart from God's truth. The Bible presents these people in seven categories:

1. *Self-deceived.* Some false teachers may be sincere, but they are still wrong. They have deceived themselves into believing their messages are true. As Jeremiah points out, their messages come psychologically from within their own minds and are not from God.

2. *Liars.* Some false prophets are deliberate liars who have no intention of telling the truth. The apostle John says, "Who is the liar? It is the man who denies that Jesus is the Christ. Such a man is the antichrist—he denies the Father and the Son" (1 John 2:22).

3. *Heretics.* These are those who preach heresy (false doctrine) and divide the church. Of them John said, "They went out from us, but they did not really belong to us" (1 John 2:19). The apostle Peter said, "There will be false teachers among you. They

will secretly introduce destructive heresies. . . .
These men blaspheme in matters they do not
understand" (2 Peter 2:1,12).

4. *Scoffers.* There are some who do not necessarily
promote false teaching so much as they outright
reject the truth of God. Of them the Bible warns,
"In the last days scoffers will come, scoffing and following their own evil desires" (2 Peter 3:3). The
apostle Paul calls them "lovers of themselves . . .
boastful, proud" (2 Timothy 3:2). Jude calls them
"grumblers and faultfinders" (Jude 16).

5. *Blasphemers.* Those who speak evil of God, Christ,
the Holy Spirit, the people of God, the kingdom of
God, and the attributes of God are called blasphemers. Jude calls them godless men who "speak abu-
sively against whatever they do not understand. . . .
They are clouds without rain . . . trees, without
fruit. . . . They are wild waves of the sea . . . wan-
dering stars" (Jude 10,12,13). The apostle Paul says
that he himself was a blasphemer before his conversion to Christ (1 Timothy 1:13).

6. *Seducers.* Jesus warned that some false prophets
will appear with miraculous signs and wonders to
seduce or deceive the very elect, "if that were possible" (Mark 13:22). Our Lord's implication is that
spiritual seduction is a very real threat even to
believers. This would account for the fact that a few
genuine but deceived believers may be found
among the cults.

7. *Reprobates.* This term means "disapproved," "de-
praved," or "rejected." Paul refers to those who have

rejected the truth of God and turned to spiritual darkness. Consequently, God has given them over to a "reprobate mind" (Romans 1:28 KJV). They have so deliberately rejected God that they have become "filled with every kind of wickedness" (verse 29). As a result, they are "God-haters" (verse 30), whose behavior is "senseless, faithless, heartless, ruthless" (verse 31). These people are so far gone spiritually that they know it and don't care. In Jesus' own prophetic message, the Olivet Discourse, He warned, "Watch out that no one deceives you. . . . Many will turn away from the faith. . . . And many false prophets will appear and deceive many people. . . . For false Christs and false prophets will appear and perform great signs and miracles" (Matthew 24:4,10,11,24). Our Lord warned His disciples of the possibility of spiritual seduction by false prophets.

The Master of Deceit

The Bible describes Satan as the "father of lies" (John 8:44) and pictures him as the ultimate deceiver. His name means "accuser," and he is depicted as the accuser of God and His people (Revelation 12:10). He is opposed to God and seeks to alienate people from the truth. He misled the fallen angels (Revelation 12:3,4). He tempts men and women to sin against God's laws (Genesis 3:1-13; 1 Timothy 6:9). He denies and rejects the truth of God and deceives those who perish without God (2 Thessalonians 2:10). Ultimately, he inspires the false prophets and the very spirit of Antichrist (1 John 2:18-23).

The Bible clearly warns us that in the last days people will "abandon the faith and follow deceiving ['seducing,' KJV] spirits and things ['doctrines,' KJV] taught by demons" (1 Timothy 4:1). These false teachings will come through hypocritical liars whose minds have been captured by

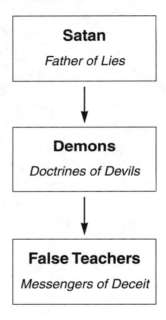

Satan's lies (1 Timothy 4:2). Thus, the process of spiritual deception is clearly outlined in Scripture:

The term *angel* (Greek, *angelos*) means "messenger." God's angels are His divine messengers (Hebrews 1:14; Revelation 1:1), and His true prophets and preachers are called the angels of the churches (Revelation 2:1,8,12,18; 3:1,7,14). By contrast, Satan is pictured as a fallen angel, the leader of other fallen angels, who deceives the world (Revelation 12:9). He is revealed as the ultimate power behind the Antichrist and the False Prophet who deceives mankind with false religion (Revelation 13:14,15). Thus, the messengers (angels) of deceit are Satan-inspired false prophets and teachers whose messages are the very spirit of Antichrist.

A century ago, A.T. Pierson, the Bible teacher who often spoke for Charles Spurgeon at the Metropolitan Tabernacle in London, wrote, "Evil spirits acquire their greatest power from their subtilty. They are *masters of the art of deception*, and aim to counterfeit that which is good rather than suggest what is obviously and wholly evil."[1]

Spiritual Deception

The lure of false doctrine is that it presents itself as the truth. It appears as a corrective measure to established doctrine. It is propagated by those who are certain they have discovered some new revelation of truth or a better interpretation of old, established truth. Either way, they are convinced they are right and everyone else is wrong.

This is Satan's oldest trick. He appeals to our self-conceit and leads us into self-deceit. When he first approached Eve, Satan questioned the integrity of God's command and appealed to her selfish desire to be like God—the same desire that led to his own fall. And there is something selfish enough in all of us to want to believe that we can know what no one else knows. C.S. Lewis said,

> What Satan put into the heads of our remote ancestors was the idea that they could "be like gods." . . . Out of that hopeless attempt has come nearly all that we can call human history . . . the long terrible story of man trying to find something other than God which will make him happy."[2]

One does not have to look hard to find expressions of self-centeredness in most cult leaders: Father Divine said he was God. David Koresh claimed to be Jesus Christ. Sun Myung Moon says he is "Lord of the Universe." Joseph Smith claimed to receive angelic revelations. Mary Baker Eddy believed her book *Key to the Scriptures* was inspired of God. Herbert W. Armstrong claimed his church was the only one on earth proclaiming "the very same gospel that Jesus taught and proclaimed."

Once the false teacher falls into the *illusion* that he or she alone is God's messenger and has a corner on His truth, spiritual deception is inevitable. Mary Baker Eddy, the founder of Christian Science, was so convinced she was right that she said, "Today the healing power of Truth is widely demonstrated as an imminent, eternal science. . . . [Its] coming as was promised by the Master, is for its establishment as a permanent dispensation among men."[3] She actually believed her "discovery" of Christian Science fulfilled the promise of Jesus' second coming.

In the preface to *Key to the Scriptures,* Mrs. Eddy said of herself, "Since the author's discovery of the might of Truth in the treatment of disease as well as of sin, her system has been fully tested and has not been found wanting."[4] It is difficult to imagine the sincerity of such self-conceit and spiritual arrogance. The only logical explanation is that she really thought she was right.

Ultimate Darkness

Once spiritual deception sets in, it leads to spiritual darkness. It is not long before the deceived cult leader begins to espouse heretical doctrine. Since he or she acknowledges no one else as God's spokesperson, traditional and orthodox concepts may be challenged or even disregarded. Charles Russell, the forefather of the Jehovah's Witnesses, was so convinced he was correct about the date of the second coming of Christ (1914) that he became equally convinced of other unorthodox beliefs as well: He denied the trinity, the deity of Christ, the personality of the Holy Spirit, the existence of hell, and the visible return of Christ.

Pride and arrogance are the sins that lead a person to become spiritually deceived. These sins take us to the second stage of spiritual deception. Satan tempts us with our own self-centeredness and lures us into spiritual darkness with the bait of our own pride. We really want to believe we are right and everybody else is wrong. The Bible calls this the "pride of life" (1 John 2:16 KJV).

Having been hooked by our arrogance, we are reeled in by our ignorance. Most people who fall into the trap of false doctrine are ignorant of the implications of other views. Hank Hanegraaff illustrates this in his epic work *Christianity in Crisis.*[5] Hanegraaff states that many sincere preachers get off the theological track because they don't know enough theology to realize their errors.

The real problem comes when false teachers love their erroneous teaching to the point they will not repent of it even when their error is exposed. This is what leads to spiritual darkness. The willful rejection of the truth results in the mind being blinded by Satan. The Bible says, "They are darkened in their understanding and separated from the life of God because of the ignorance that is in them due to the hardening of their hearts" (Ephesians 4:18).

Scripture further explains that Satan himself is the source of spiritual darkness: "The god of this age has blinded the minds of unbelievers, so that they cannot see the light of the gospel of the glory of Christ, who is the image of God" (2 Corinthians 4:4). Thus, Joseph Smith belligerently defied all appeals to rethink his theology of men becoming gods, of marital polygamy being acceptable, or his supposed angelic revelations of The Book of Mormon.

Once theological error falls into "ecclesiastical cement" it is virtually impossible to eliminate it. When false doctrine is accepted by an organized religious body it will be perpetrated by a false defense (apologetic) based upon a false premise. If I honestly believe my dog is a reincarnation of my Uncle Joe, I will look for every possible proof of Uncle Joe's personality in my dog's behavior. When a whole group of followers accept false doctrine as truth, they will organize it, categorize it, and systematize it. But that doesn't make it true!

For example, if I start driving north from Atlanta on I-75, but I really believe I'm heading south, I am not going to end up in Florida no matter what I think. The spiritually deceived person can believe Jesus returned in 1914, or moved into the heavenly temple in 1844, or that He is coming back this year. But just believing it doesn't make it so. My faith has to be anchored in the truth if it is going to do me any good.

Since Jehovah's Witnesses deny the deity of Christ, they have to reinterpret every passage of Scripture that contradicts their false doctrine (for example, John 1:1). Mormons believe that Jews came to America long before Columbus and that millions of "Nephites" and "Lamanites" once lived on the American continent hundreds of years ago. Therefore, Mormon archaeologists keep looking desperately for any material evidence of these ancient peoples to verify the historicity of their theology.

Apostate Religion

Jesus spoke often of false prophets and spiritual deception. He told His disciples that spiritual truth could be recognized by its fruits. Then he added, "Not everyone who says to me, 'Lord, Lord,' will enter the kingdom of heaven. . . . Many will say to me on that day, 'Lord, Lord, did we not prophesy in your name, and in your name drive out demons and perform many miracles?' Then I will tell them plainly, 'I never knew you. Away from me, you evildoers!' " (Matthew 7:21-23).

False religion can arise from any source. Hindu-based cults have produced an endless stream of gurus who claim to be avatars (incarnations of deity). Sai Baba says he is the living incarnation of both Jesus and Krishna! Extremist Muslims exist, such as Sheik Oman Abdel-Rahman, the deported cleric whose followers car-bombed the World Trade Center in New York City. Theirs is a gospel of hatred, violence, and murder in the name of God. Jewish Lubavitchers still believe the late Menachem Schneerson is the Messiah and are awaiting his return.

One might expect false prophets and extremist cults to arise from non-Christian religions that reject Jesus Christ. But when false cults arise from within Christianity, it is especially disturbing. The New Testament is filled with warnings about heretics, false prophets, and false prophecies. Even in apostolic times, John wrote, "Dear children, this is the last hour; and as you have heard that the antichrist is coming, even now many antichrists have come. . . . They went out from us, but they did not really belong to us" (1 John 2:18,19).

One only has to consider the fiery finale of the Branch Davidian cult led by David Koresh to see the powerful influence of false doctrine. Koresh convinced his followers that he alone could properly interpret the seven seals of the book of Revelation. By "opening" the seals, he further convinced them that he was the Lamb of God—Jesus Christ in the flesh. Therefore, his conflicts with law enforcement agencies were setting the stage for the final battle—Armageddon. He was so self-centered, *Newsweek* noted, "he was consumed by Armageddon and his role in it."[6]

Arguments may persist for some time as to whether the inferno was the result of a mass suicide, an accident, or an act of desperate self-destruction. But the whole terrible mess was the end result of a false prophet whose deceived followers perished for a lie.

It is never the will of God to defend the faith with guns and bullets. Peter attempted to defend Jesus from arrest by the Roman soldiers in the garden of Gethsemane. Our Lord told Peter to put away his sword because "all who draw the sword will die by the sword" (Matthew 26:52). Later, when Pilate questioned Jesus about being a king, the Lord replied, "My kingdom is not of this world. If it were, my servants would fight to prevent my arrest" (John 18:36).

A false prophet is one who contradicts the true message of Christ, as well as one whose predictions fail to come true. David Koresh was guilty on both counts. A typically self-deceived extremist cult leader, Koresh perished with nearly 90 of his followers in the flames at Ranch Apocalypse. But in Matthew 23:25-33, Jesus Christ warned there is a worse fate for false teachers: They will not escape the fires of hell!

The Cultic Mind

The general public was shocked when the author of an academic bestseller argued that modern students have now abandoned rational inquiry for relativism, replacing reason with emotion.[7] Today's students, he observed, don't care what is right or wrong so long as it works. They are more interested in pursuing the good life than in making right decisions. Students who are a product of modern education are not committed to noble ideas and therefore are incapable of developing noble goals.[8] Since relativity prevails, students are robbed of their spiritual values and are left with an overload of information that cannot change their lives.[9]

It is into this moral and intellectual vacuum that the cults make their greatest appeal to today's generation. They appear to offer answers to life's questions. They provide a structure for moral choices, and they demand allegiance to a great cause. But, unlike genuine Christianity, the cults recruit through deception and hold their converts by manipulation. Just try to get the guy selling flowers at the airport and other public places to tell you to which group he belongs. He won't do it. Ask those inviting you to a Bible study or campus group to tell you up front with whom or what they are associated. If they hesitate or are vague, they probably have something to hide.

In his powerful and insightful book *Unholy Devotion: Why Cults Lure Christians,* Harold Bussell makes these crucial observations about false cults:[10]

> 1. *They gain control of their followers by demanding that they surrender control of their lives.* This surrender is to be done to the cult itself in order to meet one's needs and accomplish one's goals. This is generally done under the guise of surrendering all to some higher being. In occult circles, the ultimate surrender is to Satan himself!

2. *Their manipulation bases its appeal more on emotion than logic.* Bussell notes that people today are more persuaded by the dynamics of a speaker's personality or delivery than they are by the content of his message. This means that even well-educated people can be easily manipulated by powerful appearances, dynamic messages, and emotional experiences.

3. *They offer strict guidelines for acceptable behavior.* To a morally bankrupt and confused society, most cults offer very rigid guidelines for moral behavior. The cults demand allegiance to a code of conduct that locks the followers into the group. Since no one else makes such demands, it is assumed they must be right. Following that logic, the cult can demand almost anything from its followers, who will give up everything to satisfy the convictions of the cult.

4. *They often excuse the behavior of their leaders.* The rigid demands of cults are so difficult to maintain that even their leaders often fall short. But instead of honest admissions, true confessions, or genuine repentances, the cults often try to excuse or cover up their leaders' failures. Mormons don't want to talk about Joseph Smith's polygamy. Jehovah's Witnesses never mention Charles Russell's divorce. And nobody at the Jim Jones' People's Temple talked about those Kool-Aid communion services until it was too late!

The ultimate hook of the cultic mentality is that of perpetual obligation. The cultist is never free from the cult. The assurance of salvation is never fully realized. The devotee must pray better, witness more, meditate longer, try harder, and work endlessly. Promoters of false religion leave their followers in total dependence upon themselves. They are devoid of any theological structure or biblical truth that offers a sure and lasting salvation.

David Breese makes the insightful observation in his book *The Marks of a Cult* that cultists are kept in hopeless bondage to the cult.[11] He observes that Jehovah's Witnesses are never quite sure if they are one of the 144,000. New Agers who believe in reincarnation are never sure whether they are coming back or going on ahead to something better. Krishna devotees live in constant fear of losing their Krishna-consciousness and failing to merge with deity.

Breese comments, "A thoughtful person who examines the preaching and writing of the cults carefully is almost certain to sense a frustrating indefiniteness. He is being strung along, beguiled up a primrose path to nowhere."[12] In contrast to the uncertainty of the cultic appeal, consider the striking words of the apostle Paul, who said, "I know whom I have believed, and am persuaded that he is able to keep that which I have committed unto him against that day" (2 Timothy 1:12 KJV).

The Big Lie

Most cults bind their converts by the lie that they alone have the truth and, therefore, they are the only true people of God. Tragically, this idea often begins with sincere self-deception. Many cult leaders actually believe they have discovered the truth that others fail to see. Therefore they quickly conclude they are the only ones who know the truth.

Once the cultist buys the lie that "we" alone are right and all others are wrong, spiritual pride and arrogance set in quickly. Since the cult alone has the truth, it can judge all other beliefs as erroneous. All they have to do is evaluate the claims of others in comparison with their own beliefs. Any discrepancy is viewed as a departure from the truth (as understood by the cult). Detractors are quickly denounced as heretics, liars, and deceivers.

The acceptance of the lies that "we alone are God's people" and "we alone know the truth" leads to the abandonment of one's self to the exaggerated claims of the cult leader ("I am God" or "I alone can lead you to God"). This, in turn, immerses the devotee into the mind-set of the cult, which becomes his or her new world.

Each cult has a vocabulary unique to itself. The longer the convert is isolated by the group, the more he or she will begin to think and talk in the terminology of the cult. In time, new concepts fill one's conversations: "holy discourses," "heavenly handshake," "dreamless sleep," "the force," "spirit guides," "heavenly deception," "according to principle," "spoiling the system," "harmonic convergence," "karma," "mantras," "millennial dawn," "Nephites," "telestial Kingdom," "devas," "mahatmas," "flirty fishing," and "animal magnetism" become designations, code words, and shibboleths used by cult insiders.

Unfortunately, most cult evangelists don't begin by emphasizing the unique and bizarre elements of their cult's doctrine. Rather, they tend to start with commonly used religious terminology. Many talk of finding inner peace, spiritual help, and personal salvation. Mormons are big on morality and family. Jehovah's Witnesses are concerned about Bible prophecy and appeal to one's need to understand the future. Christian Scientists emphasize the power of the mind, which tends to appeal to intellectuals. New Agers want to help you find yourself by finding their concept of God.

The Final Trap

All this may sound rather harmless at first, but it becomes the hook that lures the potential convert into the cultic world. The extremist cults then take total control of the convert's life. Some insist that all one's possessions be donated to the cause. Some determine whom you can marry, where you can live, and what time you should get up in the morning. The more general cults allow members to possess their own property, live in their own homes, and make their own daily decisions. But they also tend to exert strong control through guilt manipulation, personal intimidation, and even social rejection and shunning.

The cult member ends up being intimidated by such threats only because he or she has already believed it! The acceptance of the basic cult lie ("we alone are God's true people") leads to uncritical allegiance to leadership ("I am God's only true spokesperson"), and the rest is automatic! Hence, Moonies believe demons sit on their eyelids to make them sleep during lectures because that is what their leaders teach.[13] Many New Agers believe they are reincarnations of famous people because their leaders believe it about themselves.[14] Jehovah's Witnesses won't salute the flag or serve in the military because their leaders believe that Christ has already returned and set up His kingdom, which supersedes all human governments. Believing the Church Age to have ended in 1914, they meet in kingdom halls and denounce all churches as apostate.

Once you accept the premise of false teaching, all the rest falls consistently in line. Believing the basic lie, one closes his mind to the truth and throws away the key of logic. From that point on, anything and everything can and will make sense to the cultic mentality—even worshiping the Antichrist!

The fact that false prophets have been on the rise for the past 100 years would seem to indicate that Satan's final deception is almost complete. The stage is set for the ultimate False Prophet to perpetuate the final deception.

4

The Darkness of Our Times

But mark this: There will be terrible times in the last days.

—2 Timothy 3:1

The spiritual vacuum of our times is being filled with the darkness of evil. We are no longer a predominantly Christian society. The symbols and trappings of Christianity remain, but the heart and soul of it have been polluted by the secular pursuit of life without God. More and more, it is evident that the majority of people are looking in all the wrong places to find meaning and purpose to their lives.

Aleksandr Solzhenitsyn has remarked, "The forces of Evil have begun their decisive offensive."[1] So it seems that we are digging in for what may well be the final onslaught against biblical Christianity. The final blow may not come from a direct offensive of anti-Christian sentiment, but from sheer neglect of its message. After all, what better way to undermine the gospel than to live as though it did not exist?

We see evidence of that neglect in every form of art, music, literature, and film. Many of the artists and writers are void of spiritual values, conflicts, and concerns. They are so ignorant of biblical truth that they go about their lives as if there were no God. The movies are full of characters like the one portrayed by Michael Douglas in *Wall Street*, who bellows out: "Greed is good! Greed works!" Then there is the proverbial prostitute characterized by Julia Roberts in *Pretty Woman*, who defends her profession with the inane remark, "You gotta make a living."

These are just a few of the many examples of non-Christian or even anti-Christian sentiment which predominate modern culture. There are still many genuine believers who have not capitulated to secularism, materialism, and pragmatism. But all too often, these attitudes can be found even within the Christian community. It is as though the darkness is so great that even we can't always find our way through the maze of modern life.

We have every convenience conceivable to make our lives easier. Jet airplanes speed us across the country and around the world in a matter of hours. Satellite television transmissions bring world events to us within seconds. Air conditioning cools us in the summer; central heating warms us in the winter. Life is no longer a struggle for raw survival. It is often the pursuit of life, liberty, and happiness just as our forefathers planned.

But the freedom to pursue life often allows us to become sidetracked from its true meaning and purpose. Most people are so busy these days that they can't sit still long enough to enjoy the life they have. Most of us overextend and overcommit ourselves to the point that even our leisure time often increases our stress.

The New Dark Ages

Charles Colson has noted that the church had to stand alone against the barbarian culture of the Dark Ages.[2] Classical Rome had become corrupt from within and fell to the waves of warring bands of illiterate barbarian tribes. Medieval Europe lay in the shambles of spiritual darkness, but the church fought illiteracy, moral degradation, and political corruption. The barbarians could not withstand the stubborn resistance of Christian civilization. In time, Europe emerged from the Dark Ages into an era of spiritual and intellectual creativity and growth.

Colson sees the church at the same crisis point today—confronting the new Dark Ages. The Bible predicts that a time of spiritual apostasy will precede the revealing of the Antichrist ("man of sin").[3] The book of Revelation describes this apostasy as the religion of the "great whore." She is the epitome of false religion and spiritual adultery. By contrast, the New Testament church is pictured as a virgin betrothed to Christ.

Most Evangelicals believe this apostasy is made up of people who outwardly profess Christianity but have no inward possession of the Spirit of God. Peter Lalonde argues that the apostate whore is not made up of any particular denomination, but of "all those who do not truly love the Lord."[4] Many view the false religion of the last days as a combination of corrupted Roman Catholicism, liberal Protestantism, New Age mysticism, and materialistic Evangelicalism all rolled into one grand deception.

Years ago, professing Christians almost always acknowl-edged the authority of Scripture. Whether they were willing to live by it or not, people believed the legitimacy of biblical morality. Today, that is often not the case. Even professing Evangelical believers will often disregard the commands of God. It is not unusual today for people to respond with an "I don't care" attitude when confronted with biblical truth. People used to say, "Pastor, I know what I'm doing is wrong, but I just can't help myself." Today, the more common response is, "I know what the Bible says, but I'm going to do what I want to do anyway."

This shift of attitude betrays the selfism that is so preva-lent in our modern culture. People want what is best for themselves regardless of who they hurt or what moral prin-ciples they violate.

Spirit of Antichrist

There is no doubt in my mind that the stage is already set for the final rise of apostasy. The apostle John warned centuries ago that the spirit of Antichrist is already at work through the lust of the flesh, the lust of the eyes, and the pride of life. He added that there are "many antichrists" who "went out from us" because they "did not belong to us" (1 John 2:16-19; 4:1-4).

Professing Christians who really do not know Christ and do not possess His Spirit are called little antichrists because they express the spirit and attitude of Antichrist. But they only *prefigure* the Antichrist, who is described in the Bible as the "man of sin," the "son of perdition," and the "beast out of the sea."

The idea that such a great deceiver could come upon the world scene instantly and dramatically may seem remote to some, but many New Agers have already proposed such a possibility. Barbara Marx Hubbard, executive director of the World Future Society and a Democratic Party nominee for vice president of the United States in 1984, believes that a mass transformation could trigger a "planetary Pentecost" that would empower millions of people at once in a quantum leap toward world wholeness.[5] Hubbard sees this as "the great instant of cooperation" that will be triggered by some great cosmic event.

Many Evangelicals believe the rapture of the church will be just such an event! It will have global significance and proportions that will shake the entire world population. Thus, it will have to be explained in some manner. The Bible warns that explanation will be a lie that brings "powerful delusion" to the unbelieving world (2 Thessalonians 2:11). Whether New Age prophecies are setting the stage for this deception, only time will tell. But the mindset of New Age thinking certainly comes dangerously closer to this than anything we have seen before.

Left Behind

While the anticipation of Christ's coming to rapture the church is the blessed hope of the believer, it is a sobering matter for those who are left behind. They are described as the deceived unbelievers who have no hope. They will succumb to the great lie and will perish and be damned (2 Thessalonians 2:10-12). This is not a pretty picture, but it is God's warning to a defiant and unbelieving world.

When the Antichrist rises to power, he will oppose God, exalt himself above God, and even claim to be God (2 Thessalonians 2:4). The Bible warns us that the Antichrist will be empowered by Satan to do miracles of signs and wonders (2 Thessalonians 2:9). He will be assisted by the False Prophet who encourages the worship of the Antichrist as God.

The description of the reign of the Antichrist in biblical prophecy indicates a one-world system in the final days. The Antichrist will deceive the world and control the world's economy. Thus, no one can buy or sell except those who have "the mark, which is the name of the beast or the number of his name" (Revelation 13:17). Those who are left behind at the rapture are caught in the global system and cannot escape.

This entire period of time is described as the tribulation. It is a time of trouble for the whole world. The Bible predicts that during this time a third of the trees and all of the grass will be burned up. It predicts air pollution, water pollution, earthquakes, war, and total chaos (see Revelation 6:12-14; 8:7-12). At least one-third of mankind will die during this time (Revelation 9:15).

Being left behind for most people means they will be deceived and never come to true faith in Christ. It means being trapped in the global empire of the satanic forces of the Antichrist and the False Prophet. Peter Lalonde observes:

> Regardless of the way the Antichrist rises to power, and regardless of the exact nature of the signs and wonders that accompany his rise, we know that he will accomplish three main objectives. First, he will convince the Jews that he is their long-awaited Messiah. Secondly, he will convince the false church that is left behind after the rapture that he is the true Christ. Finally, he will convince everyone that this is actually the beginning of the millennial

period . . . during which people live together in peace and harmony for a thousand years.[6]

We can only guess how and when this deception will begin to occur. But even the most skeptical mind must admit that our concepts of truth and reality have changed drastically in the past 50 years. People are no longer concerned about what is true; rather, they want to know what works for them.

The powerful and revealing book *The Agony of Deceit,* edited by Michael Horton, provides vivid details of the erroneous and even heretical ideas being promoted by some extremist television preachers.[7] The tragedy of our times is that even well-intentioned believers are often caught up in doctrinal error and don't even know it. Every human being is vulnerable to error, but when the ultimate deception comes, few will be able to withstand it.

Yes, some people will still come to faith in Christ during the tribulation, but they will be martyred for their beliefs. This present age is no time to gamble with your future or your eternal destiny. Those who are left behind at the rapture will witness the rise of the Antichrist, his false promise of peace, his persecution of believers, and his eventual war with God.

Whose Fault Is It?

The Roman orator Cicero once said, "It is impossible to know the truth and not be held responsible." Yet today we find millions of Americans who realize something has gone wrong in our country, but they have not taken the initiative to find out what it is or what to do about it. Too many Americans blame the politicians for the sad state of affairs we are in today, but it is we, the American people, who have allowed these conditions to exist. Many have protested pornography, homosexuality, abortion, and other moral and social ills, yet they still permeate our society. The real root of our national decay is moral and spiritual. This has resulted in decadence in every area of American life—economics, business, politics, and public life in general.

Over a decade ago, Marvin Stone observed the growing trend of callousness in our society. He observed: "We shrug off almost everything now, moving on to the next fleeting titillation. It's as if we are beyond making distinctions, beyond caring. . . . After two centuries we have reached a consensus of indifference."[8]

The real tragedy of our times is that people have almost totally neglected the spiritual values that made our country great, while pursuing the temporal and material values that can never bring lasting satisfaction to the human soul. Man was created in the image of God with a god-consciousness. Ultimately, we can only be satisfied by knowing, loving, and serving God. Every other approach to life degenerates into the mindless pursuit of self-interest and self-gratification.

Drug-addiction and alcoholism are still prevalent in our society. People are spending their lives and their money lusting after things that can never satisfy their deepest needs. We live in a twisted world of depressed people who have violated divine laws and are now suffering the consequences of guilt, confusion, and emptiness.

Is There Any Hope?

Sin is the transgression of God's law. When a person does what is right in his own eyes, he is really saying that it does not matter to him what God thinks about it. The Bible reminds us, "Righteousness exalts a nation, but sin is a disgrace to any people" (Proverbs 14:34). People or nations cannot ignore God's laws, live as they please, and expect to be happy and blessed. This does not mean that God gloats in His judgments, because He does not. God's heart is broken over our sins, and His punishments are meant to correct us and bring us to repentance.

God gave Israel a wonderful promise: "If my people, who are called by my name, will humble themselves and pray and seek my face and turn from their wicked ways, then will I hear from heaven and will forgive their sin and will heal their land" (2 Chronicles 7:14). As Christians living at the dawn of the twenty-first century, we must again repent and turn to God, believing that He will forgive our sins and heal our land.

Many have forgotten God's gracious intervention. Others have neglected their promises to God. The time has come for another clarion call to revival among God's people. Our political leaders may help or hinder that process, but the future of America is not in their hands. God's people are the only ones who can make a lasting difference, and that not of ourselves but by the grace of God. As the Lord directs and guides us, we can be the light of the world in a time of spiritual darkness.

Taking a Stand

It is never popular to stand against the trends of the time, but that is exactly what we are often called to do. If Bible-believing Christians are not willing to stand up for biblical morality, who will?

Human life is precious to God. Jesus Christ died upon the cross for every human being. The Christian heritage in

America has emphasized the dignity of human life. We have been known as a nation that honors and protects the right to life, but our national tolerance of abortion is causing us to lose respect for the sanctity of life. More babies have been legally murdered by abortion since 1973 than the total number of Americans killed in all the wars in our nation's history.

Ironically, many of those who defend and promote abortion are the very same people who turn right around and want to protect baby whales, spotted owls, wolves, and eagles' eggs. Only a morally perverted society would value animal life above human life. Certainly we ought to be concerned about the natural environment. I believe we ought to do all we can to prevent the extinction of various species—but not at the expense of human life! Abortionists will never convince me that I should be more concerned about a baby whale than a baby boy or girl.

The searing of the American conscience on the issue of abortion only opens the door to further atrocities like infanticide and euthanasia. Dr. C. Everett Koop, former U.S. Surgeon General, and the late Dr. Francis Schaeffer put it this way: "Once the uniqueness of people as created by God is removed . . . there is no reason not to treat people as things to be experimented on. . . . If people are not unique, as made in the image of God, the barrier is gone. . . . Will a society which has assumed the right to kill infants in the womb—because they are unwanted, imperfect, or merely inconvenient—have difficulty in assuming the right to kill other human beings, especially older adults who are judged unwanted, imperfect, or a social nuisance?"[9]

It is a known fact of history that Adolph Hitler ordered the abortion of babies whose expectant mothers had a history of genetic defects long before he began the genocide of the Jews whom he considered genetically defective. Once a few people have the power to decide which life and whose life may be eliminated, anything can be legitimatized in the name of rights, freedoms, or the good of the state.

The same arguments are used to justify pornography. Under the false guise of First Amendment rights, every imaginable kind of sexual perversion has been exploited by pornographic books, magazines, and films. *Playboy* magazine brought sex into the drugstores in the 1950s. "R" and "X" rated movies brought it to the movie screens in the 1960s and 1970s. Cable television brought it into the American home in the 1980s. Today the media provides a daily menu of perversion to undermine the American family.

After so many years of this kind of exposure to sexual lust, violence, and permissiveness, it is no wonder we are in such a moral quagmire today. Sex is no longer viewed as a sacred bond between a husband and wife. Instead, it is promoted as a recreational alternative for consenting partners of any type. Women are tragically demeaned. The privacy of sex is destroyed, and true intimacy is lost.

Emptiness of Our Times

Ours has often been characterized as an empty and meaningless generation. The mindless pursuit of personal pleasure and the abandonment of God's moral laws have left millions of people desolate, desperately seeking real satisfaction in their lives. The prevailing atmosphere of sexual license has eroded the true meaning of life itself. Tragically, the basic human needs for love, acceptance, companionship, intimacy, and personal affirmation are totally lost in the pursuit of lust, sex, and perversion.

Everything that people really need spiritually and psychologically is lost when God is left out. He and He alone can fill the spiritual vacuum of the human soul. He and He alone can give us the love and acceptance we really need.

I am amazed how many people risk their marriages, their families, their jobs, their security, and their own integrity for a moment of pleasure. Their excuse is usually stated as looking for love, happiness, and acceptance. Yet, those are the very things God promises to give us. "Wasn't God enough?" I want to ask them. "Why did you think someone else could fill that void in your life if God could not?"

There is something fundamentally wrong with our culture. We have more conveniences, more technology, and more leisure time than any society has ever had, and yet most people today are not happy! When will we learn that things will not make us happy? Only God can satisfy the human heart's longing for true joy and happiness. Jesus said, "I have come that they may have life, and have it to the full" (John 10:10).

Our generation must face the fact that life only works when it is lived God's way. As long as we continue seeking the meaning and purpose of life without God, we will never find it. Only when men and women come to the end of themselves and turn to God will they find the true meaning of life.

Life without God is like being trapped in a long dark tunnel with no light. A person could grope around in the darkness for years trying to content himself with the bits and pieces of life that he might stumble upon. But in all that time, he would not find the real beauty of life until someone found him and set him free.

Many years ago, Charles Wesley, the great hymn writer, put it like this:

> Long my imprisoned spirit lay,
> Fast bound in sin and nature's night;
> Thine eye diffused a quick'ning ray,
> I woke; the dungeon flamed with light;
> My chains fell off, my heart was free;
> I rose, went forth and followed Thee.[10]

5

Dawn of the
New Millennium

*Satan himself masquerades as an
angel of light.*

—2 Corinthians 11:14

God never promised that things would get easier as we neared the end of the age. In fact, premillennarians believe that things will get worse before they get better. This does not mean, however, that they will necessarily get worse during our lifetime or that the end must come any time soon. While we anticipate the return of Christ at any moment, we must also recognize that we cannot avoid our citizenship responsibilities in the meantime.

The twentieth century has brought the most incredible changes imaginable to the human race. Automobiles, airplanes, radios, televisions, and computers have thrust us into an environment our forefathers never could have envisioned. Whether we like it or not, each one of us is affected by modern technology daily, and that technology is shaping our lives. It is no wonder that historian Paul Johnson called these days "modern times."[1]

Yet with the advancement of modernity has come a restless uneasiness about the traditional values that are slipping away from our society. At times consciously and at other times unconsciously, we seem to be discarding the very ideas that built this great society. It would even seem that we have exchanged our souls for a technological mess of pottage.

As the twentieth century sped along, secularism began to replace the Judeo-Christian values of our society. God was gradually but systematically removed from any place of prominence in our intellectual lives. Scientism emerged, turning pure science into a religion, which taught that natural laws, not spiritual principles, guided the universe.[2]

The entrenchment of the theory of evolution made God unnecessary in our culture. Many people actually felt betrayed because their belief in God had enabled them to believe in their own worth and dignity. Life had meaning and purpose as people lived to bring glory to God. But now those ideas have been swept away by the intellectual broom of secularism. Man now sees himself as little more than a glorified animal whose highest instincts are to satisfy his own selfish desires.

The Reign of Relativism

The philosophical concept that dominates the thinking of people today is *relativism*.[3] It is the opposite of absolutism and teaches that all truth is relative to its context. There are *no absolutes* according to this belief. Absolute truth is an impossibility in a world of relative contingencies. Something is "true" only because a majority of people accept it as truth; all issues are subject to human interpretation at any given point in time. In other words, what is considered to be true in one culture may not be true in another.

Relativism dethrones divine law. It not only rejects the teachings of Scripture as binding upon human behavior, but it even rejects the very concept of Scripture. According to relativism, a writing is considered scripture only because a society deems it so. The writing is not viewed as inherently divine in nature. Relativists view the Bible on the same level as the Koran, the Tripitakas of Buddha, or the Hindu Vedas. In some cases, modern critics have even suggested that other writings are superior to the Bible.

The influence of relativism has affected nearly every area of modern thinking. Once one accepts the basic premise of relativism, he no longer views truth as an absolute proposition.[4] The great danger of this concept is that it leads to a naïve acceptance of the consequences of secularism. Under this system of thought, even the concepts of good and evil are viewed as culturally conditioned, and therefore relative to the perspective of that culture. Thus, even murder is not considered inherently wrong. It is only wrong because society deems it wrong.

Have We Lost Our Minds?

One of the most powerful books to appear in recent times is *The Closing of the American Mind*.[5] Written by Allan Bloom, a professor of social thought at the University of Chicago, this blockbuster bestseller explores the intellectual vacuum of our time. Bloom argues that today's students are unlike any generation that has preceded them. They are headed, in his opinion, to intellectual oblivion because of the relativism that has permeated our culture.

Bloom calls his volume "a meditation on the state of our souls."[6] Though the book is not written from a Christian standpoint, it raises many issues Christians have been concerned about for years. Bloom argues that students have been so conditioned by our educational system to believe that all truth is relative that they are devoid of absolutes on which to build their lives. As a result, he explains, our culture has drifted with the winds of self-gratification.[7]

Bloom is especially concerned about the self-centeredness of today's students. "Students these days are, in general, nice," he says. But, he adds, "They are not particularly moral or noble." The author observes that they are the product of good times when "neither tyranny nor want has hardened them or made demands on them." As a result, he warns that young people today have abandoned themselves to the pursuit of the "good life."[8]

Unfortunately, the current quest of most students is for money, sex, power, and pleasure. It should not surprise us that these are problems for Christians as well because they are the dead-end options of a society stuck on itself.

Bloom writes, "Country, religion, family, ideas of civilization, all the sentimental and historical forces that stood between cosmic infinity and the individual, providing some notion of a place within the whole, have been rationalized away and have lost their compelling force."[9] He also adds that we are now experiencing what de Tocqueville, the French admirer of American democracy, warned would ultimately lead to the "disappearance of citizens and statesmen." In other words, everybody is caught up in "making it" for himself and really isn't interested in the common good of others.

The rise of *individualism,* coupled with the decline of the traditional family, has left us with a generation that has a tough time making commitments. This tendency shows up in almost every area of life, from choosing a career, to holding a job, to getting married. Reluctance to commit oneself to a belief or ideal is the inevitable result of relativism in our culture. We have a situation akin to the days of the biblical judges, when "every man did that which was right in his own eyes."

Going First Class on the Titanic

Another educator, Arthur Levine, has described the current student mentality as that of going "first class on the Titanic."[10] What he means is that students not only have become self-centered, but they have also given up any real hope of solving the world's problems. They view society as a sinking ship that will never reach its ultimate destination; they view themselves as stuck on a hopeless voyage. Since they can't get off, they simply clamor for the first-class seats on the top deck so they can enjoy the ride until disaster strikes. In other words, if they are going to be stuck on the *Titanic*, they intend to make the best of it.

Whether we like it or not, most of us are products of our times. As Christians, we must literally fight against the undercurrent of secularism and relativism that is sweeping away our Judeo-Christian foundation. Today's Christian students must be willing to swim upstream against the intellectual tide if they hope to make any real difference in our society. Claiming to be a Christian really isn't enough anymore; we must we willing to show it.

The choices we make regarding the investment of our lives will reflect whether we are committed to ourselves or others. In a time when most people are choosing to live for themselves, we must be willing to demonstrate the reality of Christ by living for Him and investing ourselves in others. This is the real key to finding meaning and purpose in one's life.

The Appeasement of Evil

The greatest danger of relativism is that it leads to the eventual appeasement of evil. If all truth is relative, then no belief is worth dying for. If I have part of the truth and you have part of the truth, then neither of us has the whole truth. Once we accept this concept, we have no basis upon which to judge actions as morally right or wrong. Thus, it should not surprise us that secular society is willing to tolerate abortion, euthanasia, and even infanticide. The unborn, the elderly, the retarded, and the handicapped all become expendable by such logic.[11]

Former Surgeon General C. Everett Koop calls this indifference to the sanctity of life the "slide to Auschwitz."[12] Once philosophers, theologians, and medical personnel adopt such a view, a growing loss of human dignity will automatically occur. This is the same intellectual journey that led to the acceptance of Hitler's Nazi atrocities. A change in the moral climate toward human life is all that is necessary for the systematic elimination of undesirable life forms to become the norm.

Australian ethicist Peter Singer recently said, "We can no longer base our ethics on the idea that human beings are a special form of creation, made in the image of God, singled out from all other animals, and alone possessing an immortal soul."[13] Commenting on Singer's statement, Cal Thomas observes that removing the protective layer of man's uniqueness leaves him as vulnerable as a dog or a pig in the discussion about who or what ought to live—an assertion that Singer himself makes![14]

In commenting on the seriousness of abortion, Stuart Briscoe says, "Destruction of that made in the image of God challenges the divine intention. If God makes man for eternity and gives him the ability to function in relationship to Him, anyone who kills that man destroys what God had in mind. The destroyer shakes his fist in the face of God."[15]

A Humanistic View of Government

Humanism is that form of secularism that views man, not God, as the central reality of life. Gloria Steinem, founding editor of *MS* magazine and recipient of the American Humanist Association Pioneer Award, said, "By the twenty-first century we will, I hope, raise our children to believe in human potential, not God."[16] Humanists, in general, believe that people must solve their own problems apart from any divine guidance. Secular humanism and relativism are the philosophic bases of modern liberalism.

Tim LaHaye has defined secular humanism as "a God-less, man-centered philosophy of life that rejects moral absolutes and traditional values."[17] He argues that secular humanists have relentlessly sought to secularize our nation by influencing legislative and judicial governmental control in every area of our society, including the church and the family.

R.C. Sproul defines humanism as an *anthropocentric* (man-centered) view of life as opposed to a *theocentric* (God-centered) view of life.[18] He traces its origins to the pre-Socratic Greek philosopher Protagoras, whose motto was *homo mensura,* meaning "man (is) the measure." As a result of its own presuppositions, humanism rejects the concept of divinely revealed moral absolutes and argues for man's right to determine his own morality.

Modern humanism, as reflected in the *Humanist Manifestos* (1933, 1973) and the *Humanist Declaration* (1980), is decidedly anti-Christian in its bias. One leading proponent of humanist education, John Dewey, said, "Religion tends to hinder the evolutionary progress of man."[19] In reality, Francis Schaeffer contended, humanism borrowed the moral concerns of Christianity and tore them loose from their theological foundation. Unless it is stopped, he warned, humanism "intends to beat to death the [Christian] base which made our culture possible."[20]

The Filtration of Ideas

The present conflict between religion and politics is not merely a political issue. Rather, it is the last wave of the conflict that has been raging between Christianity and anti-Christianity throughout this century. The first waves of this conflict were philosophical and then theological. As the philosophies of relativism and secularism began to dominate thinking in the late nineteenth century, they soon influenced theology as well. This gave rise to theological liberalism and the eventual ecclesiastical controversies between fundamentalism and modernism.[21]

As the concepts of relativism and secularism gained control of institutionalized religion, they provoked theological debate which, in turn, led to ecclesiastical power struggles to control the ideology of the mainline denominations. Thus the argumentation shifted to the issue of ecclesiastical control. When conservatives were unable to prevent liberalism from infiltrating and eventually controlling the theological institutions, they withdrew, forming new denominations and new institutions. This left liberalism entrenched in the mainline institutions. As time passed, succeeding generations of theological students became increasingly secularized so that today one cannot distinguish a liberal theological agenda from a secular one.

The influence of nearly a century of liberal preaching has now filtered down to the level of the common person in society. Popular literature, television, and movies all tend to reflect this mentality. As the liberal mind-set gained a grip on society, it also influenced the political process through legislative and judicial change. Political decisions began to reflect the values of secularism.

This process of the *filtration of ideas* was first brought to the attention of Evangelicals by the late Francis Schaeffer.[22] He viewed philosophy as the wellspring from which popular culture derived. As philosophical concepts filter down through the culture, they first affect the elite and eventually become popularized by society in general. The process works something like this:

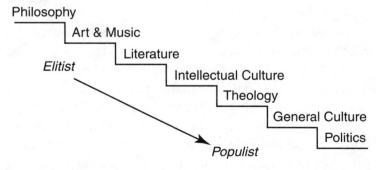

Filtration of Ideas: From intellectual elites to popular culture to politics

Schaeffer argued that the philosophical concepts of Kant and Hegel gave rise to a whole new way of thinking that resulted in relativism. He suggested that this concept spread geographically from Germany to Holland and Switzerland before it caught on in England and America. As an American living in Switzerland, Schaeffer realized that American culture was moving in the same direction as European culture, though at a slower pace. God was simply being eliminated as a serious intellectual option. Schaeffer also observed that relativism affected the intellectual classes first and was passed on to the workers by the mass media, bypassing the middle class. He observed, "The middle class was not touched by it and often is still not touched by it."[23]

The strength of the Evangelical church in America is our greatest deterrent to relativism and secularism. Were it not for the thousands of Evangelical churches and schools representing millions of members, secularism would have swept America long ago. This is why there is still a great void between Evangelical and liberal churches today. Not only does our theology differ, but our entire response to modernity rests upon totally different philosophical foundations.

What was unique about the twentieth century, however, was the ability of the mass media to translate secular values to every level of society through television, films, books, and magazines. Our inability to think critically and objectively while being entertained, especially by television, movies, or videos, leaves even the Christian community vulnerable to the influence of secularism. We can watch a program that challenges or contradicts the very values we hold dear and never even realize it!

Politics: Christianity's Last Stand

The grip of secularism on our society is so tight that its influence is being felt in nearly every area of American life. The secularization of education, morality, and public policy eventually results in the politicization of those beliefs through the legislative and judicial process. The end result will be the legalization of secularism and the disenfranchisement of Judeo-Christianity.

Politics, in the broadest sense of human governance, is the last line of defense for religion in our society. The filtration of secularism is now so nearly complete that it dares to enshrine itself through the political processes. For example, when evolutionists argued for academic freedom to present the theory of evolution in the public schools at the time of the Scopes Trial in 1925, it was assumed by both sides in the debate that creationism would also be allowed to be taught. In fact, that assumption was so widely held that no one seriously questioned it. All the evolutionists wanted at that time was the opportunity to gain a fair hearing for their position. But in the decades that passed, secularism gained such control of public education that the teaching of creation is now forbidden by law. Creationists do not even have the same fundamental academic freedom for which evolutionists once begged.[24]

A more recent example of the controversy between secularism and religion was the Civil Rights Restoration Act of 1987, popularly known as the Grove City bill. The issue involved the right of Grove City College, an Evangelical Presbyterian institution, to dismiss a homosexual staff member for violation of the church school's code of moral conduct. When initial attempts to pass the bill failed, liberal

members of Congress attached it to other proposed legislation and President Reagan vetoed it.

In the controversy that resulted, Congress was pres-
sured by various religious organizations headed by Jerry
Falwell, James Kennedy, Tim LaHaye, and James Dobson to
support the president's veto. In reaction, the American
Civil Liberties Union (ACLU) and Norman Lear's People
for the American Way took out full-page advertisements in
major newspapers and lobbied the Congress to override
the veto, which they did.

Evangelicals opposed the bill because they believed it
was an attempt by secularists to force non-Christian
morality on the Christian community. Ironically, the ads
run against this Evangelical backlash implied just the opposite! Since the bill prevented the use of federal funds to
institutions that discriminated against women, minorities,
and homosexuals, the secularists actually criticized Christians for trying to use federal funds to finance their intol-
erance, when that was not the reason for the Evangelical
reaction at all. They were trying to get the secularists to
leave them alone.

One of the peculiarities of a democracy is that it is
always in a state of flux. Any particular group can poten-
tially propose new legislation at any time. Therefore,
democracies are rarely static; there is nearly always a state
of fluidity in the exchange of ideas. Unfortunately, most
Christians tend to forget this. We think that things will continue as they have always been. As a result, we live in a naïve
moment of false security in which we have forgotten the
whole history of the world.

A Publicly Irrelevant Faith

While acknowledging his personal concerns about the illusion of political power brokering, Charles Colson admits that we have come to a time when many people are advocating a privately engaging but publicly irrelevant faith.[25] He argues that two extreme positions dominate Christian thinking on the issue of religion and politics. On the one hand, he sees a politicized faith that tends to seek political solutions to spiritual problems while neglecting the church's real spiritual mission. On the other hand, Colson observes a privatized faith that "divorces religious and spiritual beliefs from public actions."[26]

Colson observes that the political left, including mainline religion, has a "morbid fear of religion encroaching on the secular realm."[27] Evangelicals have an equally morbid fear of secularism encroaching on religious freedoms. This is exactly where the controversy between religion and secularism lies today. While mainline religion has an innate fear of imposing religious values in a pluralistic society, Evangelicals have an innate fear of allowing secularists to impose antireligious values on that society.

Colson criticized former New York Governor Mario Cuomo for a publicly irrelevant position on abortion. Colson noted that the ex-governor was a practicing Catholic who held to his church's belief that abortion is wrong. As a public official, Cuomo acknowledged in a speech at the University of Notre Dame in 1984 that he not only could not impose his views on others, but that he was under no obligation to advocate such views either. Such a position, Colson says, is "impotent to reverse the tides of secularism."[28]

Where do the extremes of privatization or politicization leave us? Unfortunately, they tend to leave us in confusion. On the one extreme are Christians who believe we must take over the government in order to enforce religious values. On the other extreme are Christians who pietistically want to avoid all public or political issues. I believe that the church can have a proper balance between these two extremes. We must become a voice of conscience to our society or forever forfeit any spiritual influence in matters of public policy. The fact that religious, spiritual, and moral issues have become a subject of political debate simply indicates how far secularism has already advanced in our society.

Drawing a Line of Defense

Much of the Evangelical involvement in political issues has been little more than drawing a line of defense against the encroachment of secularism. For the most part, Evangelicals have not advocated taking rights away from secularists or humanists. Conservatives have merely insisted that secularists not deny their rights to live by the moral values and principles they believe to be valid. For example, Evangelicals are not calling for the elimination of existing rights for anyone. They simply oppose extending those rights to include the imposition of a nonbiblical morality upon the church or church-related institutions.

If we do not draw a line of defense at this point of the debate, we will end up sacrificing everything we believe in the area of public policy. This does not mean that the church cannot survive in a hostile society. In some cases, as in ancient pagan Rome and modern atheistic communism, true Christianity has actually flourished. However, in other cases, such as under the sword of Islam, it has been eradicated.

Conservative Christians are merely calling the church to awaken to its responsibilities in this latter part of the twentieth century. There is no excuse for us to lose our religious freedoms in a democratic society. If this does happen, we will have no one to blame but ourselves. The irrelevance of a privatized pietism is as dangerous to the health of Christianity as is the apathy of a self-indulgent church.

Whether we like it or not, we have come to religion's last stand in American culture. The political debate is the final attempt of secularism to prevail over religion in our society. The implications of this debate have eternal consequences. For secularism, all human values must be understood in the present, whereas the biblical worldview is eternal. R.C. Sproul rightly observes, "This is precisely where Christianity and secularism collide. This is the point of conflict."[29] Sproul observes that "right now" counts forever in Christianity. What we do has eternal significance because our existence is related to God Himself.

The Dust of Death

At the peak of secularization in the 1960s and 1970s, theologians began to talk about synthesizing Christianity with secularism in the concept of the *death of God*. They viewed God as having surrendered His transcendence and capitulating to the secular through the incarnation of Christ. When Jesus took on humanity, the transcendent God died, they argued, leaving mankind with the pursuit of its own solutions to its problems.[30]

Sproul again observes, "The death of God, in terms of the loss of transcendence and the loss of the eternal, also means the death of man. It means that history has no transcendent goal. There is no eternal purpose."[31] Once the secular mind-set gains control of the way a society thinks, it will not be long until those thoughts are translated into political structures.

Society is losing its belief in the sanctity of life. For most of human history the law has leaned on the side that life is worth preserving. That view is now shifting, and we are moving toward the idea that a substantial number of people are better off dead. Some have observed that certain changes and practices in our society related to the rejection of creation have "created a moral climate that is supportive of the move away from a high view of life."[32]

In a dramatic courtroom scene in the television version of Jerome Laurence's *Inherit the Wind*, which was based on the famous Scopes Trial, the lawyer for the defense asks a young student whose teacher had taught him evolution, "Did evolution ever do you any harm?" The lawyer asks the boy about his general health and his ability to play baseball, implying that this belief has in no way damaged the young man. While it is true that such a belief may not affect one's athletic ability, it has in time damaged the entire fabric of our society.

Os Guinness has observed that if man is merely an animal, he may just as well live like one.[33] He states that modern man's view of himself in terms of his moral behavior irretrievably alters his view of reality. "Anything left of contemporary concepts of morality and identity will be reduced to the level of the illusory, and the implications for individuals and for civilization are far-reaching."[34] Twenty-five years ago, Guinness warned that man was headed into a period of alienation, followed by mystification and romanticism. He pointed to Nietzche's view that man is in an "ontological predicament," like being tied by a rope over an abyss. He is caught in an impossible struggle that results in the great seasickness of a world without God.[35]

It was this concept from Nietzsche that led the French existentialist Jean Paul Sartre to call his first novel *Nausea.* In it, Sartre concluded that "every existent is born without reason, prolongs itself out of weakness and dies by chance." Thus, Sartre saw life as a fundamental absurdity without God.[36]

When man faces the awfulness of naked *secularism,* Guinness argues, he retreats into a psychological mystification by which he arbitrarily attempts to assign meaning to his life by establishing norms of behavior by the consensus of the population. The end result of this process is the legitimization of one man's abnormality as freedom from another man's normality. An extreme example of this was found in the Soviet Union, when those criticizing society were sent to mental asylums for "paranoid delusions about reforming society."[37] One such accused geneticist, Zhores Medvedev, said, "If things go on like this, it will end with healthy, sane people sitting in mad houses, while dangerous mental cases will walk about freely."[38]

The final stage of the decline of Western thought is *romanticism.* This occurs when we give up the aspirations of a Judeo-Christian worldview and begin to romanticize the consequences. For example, when Judeo-Christian views of death, dying, and eternal life are eliminated secularists begin romanticizing a pragmatic and casual approach to death as the ultimate escape. Guinness also warned that this would eventually lead to a revival of the concept of reincarnation as modern man's ultimate attempt to escape the meaninglessness of nonbeing.[39]

The New Age Rage

Modern man has reached the point where he does not want to face the logical consequences of a secular world without God. But instead of repenting of his rebellion against God, he is now turning to a kind of *scientific mysticism* that has been popularized as the New Age movement.[40] Modern New Age mysticism is a combination of transcendentalism, spiritualism, oriental mysticism, and transpersonal psychology.[41] It rests upon the humanist psychology that emphasizes the elevation of personal growth as the highest good on the list of man's hierarchical needs.[42]

Twenty-first-century man has come to the ultimate conclusion that he needs hope beyond himself to solve the problems of life. His choices are relatively few indeed. He can turn to God, himself, others, nature, or a mystic collective consciousness. In reality, he only has two choices: himself or God. Ironically, man's rationalism has driven him to irrationality. Either he must accept the logical consequences of living in a world without God or he must turn to God. All other options are merely wishful thinking.

Modern Americans, however, usually find it difficult to throw God away altogether. We always seem to rely on some popular myth that Superman (or someone like him) is going to come from outer space to save the world. Unfortunately, our own scientific rationality ought to tell us this isn't so. The blatant secularist knows it isn't so and has to admit that man must solve his problems alone.

The great cause for despair in Western culture is the stark realization that man may well be closer to destroying himself than to solving his problems. Everyone born after Hiroshima knows the great horror of living in a world that could be destroyed by the very technology that has made it great. This lurks in the subconscious of everyone in our society, representing such an ugly reality that we psychologically suppress it and blank it out. In the meantime, we make nearly every decision in light of that subconscious truth and pretend it isn't so. Fantasy replaces reality and leaves us victims of our own emotions. Before we realize it, we are trapped in spiritual darkness.

6

Religion of the Future

*In later times some will abandon the
faith and follow deceiving spirits and
things taught by demons.*

—1 Timothy 4:1,2

The New Age movement is part of the great paradigm shift of our times. We are continually moving from information (objective truth) to emotion (subjective truth). This may not be the final form of the new religion, but it has certainly launched the modern era into a sea of intellectual and moral relativism. It is symptomatic of the new way of thinking that will permeate the new millennium.

The New Age movement is not a passing fad. It has been gaining momentum for three decades. It represents a cultural revolt against the spiritual void of secularism. It was not until the late 1980s that the general public became aware of the popular appeal of New Age thinking. Actress Shirley MacLaine's autobiography *Out on a Limb* and several subsequent books openly promoted New Age ideals: "I am God," reincarnation, seances, crystals, and pyramid power. In August 1987, 20,000 New Agers gathered at various "sacred sites" around the world for the Harmonic Convergence, a supposed cosmic event of great significance. By December 7, 1987, the New Age movement had made the cover of *Time* magazine.

New Age thinking is rooted in the counterculture of the 1960s. Though the hippie movement died out after the Vietnam War, its ideas remained. Elliot Miller observes that New Agers are primarily baby-boomers (born shortly after World War II) who have recycled, but not rejected, the *ideals* of the hippie counterculture:[1]

1. antimaterialism

2. utopianism

3. exaltation of nature

4. rejection of traditional morality

5. fascination with the occult

Miller refers to the New Age subculture as "another America" existing alongside the secular and religious establishments and competing with them for cultural dominance.[2] He characterizes New Agers as sincere, intelligent, optimistic, and humanitarian. Unlike traditional Eastern mystics, New Agers are positive about life and their involvement in the world. They embrace the future while promoting the ideals of global peace, economic prosperity, political unification, and ecological balance.

New Agers have been variously described as "Western mystics," "hippies come of age," "secular prosperity theologians," and "secularized spiritualists." But it is their combination of subjective spirituality and secular morality that leaves them so vulnerable to satanic influence.

Age of Aquarius

New Agers hitchhike much of their ideology on the concepts of astrology, especially the idea of the "Age of Aquarius." They believe that a spiritual age is now upon us in which many people are evolving into advanced stages of spiritual consciousness. They further believe that personal transformation must precede planetary transformation. This means that New Agers are committed to the proselytization of new converts to their cause. They are out to win people over to what some, like Marilyn Ferguson, have called "the Aquarian conspiracy."[3]

Astrologers believe that human evolution is progressing in cycles corresponding to the signs of the zodiac. Each cycle allegedly lasts about 2,000 years. Following the beliefs of astrologers, New Agers believe man is now moving from the Piscean (intellectual) Age into the Aquarian (spiritual) Age.

Constance Cumbey, a Christian attorney from Detroit, Michigan, first alerted the Evangelical community to the New Age menace in her book *The Hidden Dangers of the Rainbow* (1983). While many feel she overreacted to the conspiracy threat from the New Age movement, no one can doubt her sincerity in attempting to alert the Christian public to what she discovered in New Age books, seminars, and lectures. Even Elliot Miller admits, "There is an 'Aquarian Conspiracy'—a conscious effort by a broad-based movement to subvert our cultural establishment so that we might enter a 'New Age' based on mysticism and occultism."[4]

New Age Activism

Since the publication of Mark Satin's *New Age Politics* in 1978, it has been clear that New Age activists intend to continue promoting a political agenda for a united global community under the control of a one-world government.[5] In order to convince society of the need for this new world order, New Agers have adopted several promotional techniques:

> *Psychic healing:* Using man's inner psychic energy to heal his emotional conflicts and distress.

> *Holistic health:* Combining diet and inner dynamic force to produce a healthy and productive life.

> *Transpersonal education:* Also called holistic education, it targets public education as the medium to combine humanistic and mystical approaches to learning.

> *Values clarification:* An educational technique that emphasizes that one's values emerge from within one's self and not from external codes, such as the ten commandments.

> *Human Potential:* Thought-reform techniques promoting the use of guided imagery and visualization through organization development (O.D.) and organization transformation (O.T.) seminars. Used to bring humanistic psychology and Eastern mysticism into the workplace.

New Agers promote the basic human values as 1) survival, 2) interdependence, 3) autonomy, and 4) humanness.

This leaves little or no place for biblical Christianity. In fact, the occult connection with New Age thinking is anti-Christian. A new world order based upon New Age ideology would likely view Evangelical Christianity as bigoted, divisive, and sectarian. This could easily set the stage for "justified" persecution of Christians as rebels against the cause of world peace.

New Age Spiritism

The gasoline that drives the New Age movement is spiritism, which is the practice of communicating with departed human spirits or extrahuman intelligences through a human medium by the process of channeling. In his recent book *Channeling*, Joe Klimo claims that channeling involves a human being who is possessed by an external force, power, or personality.[6] This entity exercises control over the perceptual, cognitive, and self-reflective capacities of the person who has relinquished himself to the external force.

The Bible clearly warns against involvement with witchcraft, seances, and mediums. Deuteronomy 18:10-12, commands, "Let no one be found among you . . . a medium or a spiritist or one who consults the dead. Anyone who does these things is detestable to the LORD." The prophet Isaiah warned, "When men tell you to consult mediums and spiritists, who whisper and mutter, should not a people inquire of their God? Why consult the dead on behalf of the living?" (Isaiah 8:19). Scripture acknowledges the reality of demonic spirits and their attempts to communicate through human mediums (1 Samuel 28:6-14; Acts 16:16-19). It always presents them as evil, deceptive, and malevolent. They are channels to Satan's lies, not to God's truth.

Tune In and Beam Up

Popular channels in the modern New Age movement vary from those receiving *telepathic* messages (Alice Bailey and Helen Schucman), *full-trance* channels (Kevin Ryerson and Jack Pursel), and *incarnational* channels (J.Z. Knight and Penny Tores). Each in his or her own way claims to be delivering messages from someone or something beyond this present earthly experience. They are in essence claiming supernatural revelations of truth.

The channeling craze is "like having a telephone to God," Ryerson told Shirley MacLaine. It has caught on because it short-circuits real prayer. It involves little or no disciplined study. And it promises instant answers, inspired advice, quick solutions, and easy access to spiritual information not readily available to others.

In the first chapter of their book *Opening to Channel*, Sanaya Roman and Duane Packer introduce the reader to a welcome message from their channels, Orin and DaBen.[7] This message announces channeling as an evolutionary leap upward into spiritual unfoldment and conscious transformation. Channeling, according to Orin and DaBen, builds a bridge to a loving, meaningful higher consciousness known as the All-That-Is (or the Universal Mind).

Roman and Packer promise several benefits from channeling via the message of Orin and DaBen:

- Channeling will give you the wise teacher you seek—from within yourself.

- Your guide will be a friend who is always there to support you.

- Channeling will help you learn to love yourself more.

- Spirit guides will help you achieve new levels of personal power and spiritual growth.

- All you have to do is ask for a guide and one will come to you.

Mixing a little bit of scientific information about electromagnetic fields together with self-help psychology and occult spiritism, the seeker is left wide open to buy into the demonic realm of the spirit world. Opening your soul to channeling the psychologically induced impressions of one's so-called spirit guide plays right into the hand of Satan. Such a subjective and self-centered approach to truth leaves one the victim of "the father of lies" (John 8:44).

The New Theology

C.S. Lewis, in his masterpiece *The Screwtape Letters,* warns against producing a vaguely devotional mood of prayer that requires no real concentration on the will or intelligence. This bears only a superficial resemblance to true prayer: "That is exactly the sort of prayer we want," Screwtape advises Wormwood. The demonic uncle goes on to advise his nephew that the best way to nullify human prayer is to get people to "turn their gaze away from Him (God) toward themselves."[8]

This is precisely the danger in the New Age cults. The objective focus is shifted away from God toward self and results in some of the most incredible self-deception ever perpetrated on the general public: channeling, visualization, astral projection, altered consciousness, reincarnation, and even time travel!

In her book *Creative Visualization,* Shakti Gawain advises her readers to relax into "a deep, quiet, meditative state of mind" in order to visualize the reality that they want to create for themselves. "It is not necessary to have faith in any power outside yourself," she adds.[9] To help her readers find the power of positive affirmation, Gawain suggests they say the following:[10]

- Every day in every way I'm getting better and better.

- My life is blossoming in total perfection.

- Everything I need is already within me.

- I am the master of my life.

- It's okay for me to have everything I want!

Then she explains, "Affirmations are often most powerful and inspiring when they include references to spiritual sources. Mention of God, Christ, Buddha, or any great master adds spiritual energy to your affirmation."[11] She closes with the following examples:

- My higher self is guiding me in everything I do.

- The power of God flows through me.

- Divine love is working through me.

- I am one with my higher nature, and I have infinite creative power.

- Wherever I am, God is, and all is well!

New Age theology represents a do-it-yourself form of religion. A person can pick and choose whatever ideas, beliefs, concepts, and concerns happen to appeal to him personally. The rest can merely be set aside; they need not be rejected.

The bottom line is obvious. New Age theology rests upon pantheism. Its logical paradigm is:

> All is God,
>
> God is all,
>
> Man is part of all,
>
> Therefore, man is God.

The only thing separating man from God is his own consciousness, not his sin, New Agers believe. Thus, they propose finding God within oneself by altering one's consciousness through meditation, chanting, channeling, sensory expansion, ecstatic dancing, and even fire-walking. The New Age approach to spirituality is more a matter of experience than belief. Altered consciousness leads to self-realization, which results in personal transformation (the New Ager's form of salvation). In this process, personal experience becomes the final authority to define one's spiritual journey.

New Age Network

In his very helpful book *A Crash Course on the New Age Movement,* Elliot Miller defines the New Age movement as an informal network of individuals and organizations bound together by common values (mysticism and monism) and a common vision (coming new age of Aquarius).[12] Within the New Age network are several separate strands that interconnect:

1. *Consciousness movement:* Those advocating the expansion of human consciousness by altered mental states, resulting in the expansion of human awareness.

2. *Holistic health:* Those encouraging better food and diet for better mental and spiritual development.

3. *Human potential:* The self-help psychology of self-awareness, self-actualization, and self-improvement.

4. *Eastern mysticism:* Various gurus advocating Transcendental Meditation, astral projection, reincarnation, and various Hindu doctrines that view the material world as illusionary.

5. *Occultism:* Pseudoscientific return to witchcraft, satanism, shamans, mediums, palm readers, and tarot cards.

The blend of these various elements varies with every individual and every subgroup within the New Age network. Some lean toward ecological issues (save the planet); others lean toward global peace issues (make love, not war); and still others prefer a mystical orientation that mixes meditation, yoga, est, and astrology with a strong belief in reincarnation. The combinations of any of these elements are like fingers of an intellectual hand reaching out to potential followers.

Miller states, "New Agers tend to be eclectic: they draw what they think is the best from many sources. Long-term exclusive devotion to a single teacher, teaching, or technique is not the norm. They move from one approach to another in their spiritual quests."[13] Because there is no objective truth, the New Ager creates his or her own subjective truth.

Therefore, the uniqueness of the gospel of salvation through Jesus Christ can be easily rejected with, "That's *your* truth, but it's not for me."

It is this merging of scientific mysticism with a rejection of materialistic secularism that has resulted in New Age thinking. This thinking then couples with the Human Potential movement, which offers a number of techniques for advancing one's metaphysical evolution. The New Age transformationalists seek the total transformation of society along ideological lines consistent with their own beliefs. By challenging the "myths" of matter, time, space, and death, New Agers believe they will release our untapped human potential to create a new and better world.

The great danger in New Age thinking is its unwillingness to face the facts. There is no scientific proof for the mystical claims of reincarnation, spirit guides, astral projection, time travel, or a dozen other ideas popularized at New Age psychic fairs. When the process of mystification is complete, it leaves man dangling at the end of his own intellectual rope—with nowhere to land!

The spiritual void caused by the rejection of Christianity has left modern man desperately looking for a spiritual reality beyond himself. New Agers argue that our overemphasis on rationality has caused us to lose our intuitive awareness. Like the old Jedi warrior in *Star Wars,* New Agers advise people to let their feelings guide them. The collective "force" of humanity (past and present) will guide you better than following mere objective facts, they teach.

In the end, objectivity is thrown out the window by New Agers. In turn, they want to blame the rest of the world for its collective intellectual blindness. This leads to the great *paradigm shift,* or new way of thinking about old problems. Leading the vanguard of New Age thinkers is

Fritjof Capra, who argues that the old mechanistic perspective of the world must be replaced by the view that sees the world as one indivisible, dynamic whole whose parts are interrelated in the cosmic process.

Selling It to the Public

In order to intellectually promote the idea of a new world order, New Agers turn to mysticism as an ally. Synthesis replaces analysis of scientific data. The intuitive ability to recognize "wholes" replaces the need to analyze all the "parts." Capra states, "The systems view of life is spiritual in its deepest essence and thus consistent with many ideas held in mystical traditions."[14]

New Agers tie their concepts of an emerging world order to the concept of purposeful and creative evolution. Following the ideas of German philosopher G.W.F. Hegel, they view God as a *process* rather than a person. Thus, for New Agers, evolution is "God in process." Elliot Miller observes, "Without such faith in evolution, New Agers would be incapable of maintaining their distinctive optimism."[15]

Consequently, New Agers believe in the evolutionary emergence of a new collective consciousness that will result in a new humanity. They will solve the threats of nuclear war, ecological disaster, and economic collapse by an intuitive and mystical approach to life. New Age thinker Donald Keys put it like this: "A new kind of world—the world into which we are already moving—requires a new kind of person, a person with a planetary perspective."[16]

To make this hopeful human improvement work, New Agers propose a quantum leap forward in evolution. John White says, "We are witnessing the final phase of homo sapiens and the simultaneous emergence of what I have named Homo Noeticus, a more advanced form of humanity. .... As we pass from the Age of Ego to the Age of God, civilization will be transformed from top to bottom. A society founded on love and wisdom will emerge."[17]

All of this may seem like wishful thinking in light of the human tragedies of crime, war, drought, and starvation. But to the New Agers, it is a religion—with faith in evolution as the process and the worship of the planet as God. On this basis, New Agers call upon everyone to surrender their personal agendas to the ecological well-being of the living Earth, "Gaia." "Save the planet" is the evangelistic cry of the New Age movement.

It is this kind of mental gymnastics that enables New Agers to redefine the terms and concepts of spirituality. They are ready to accept the earth or the self as God. They believe in the existence of departed spirits, ghosts, time travelers, extraterrestrial beings, angels, demons, witches, and wizards. Their influence can be seen in movies like *Star Wars, Ghost, Field of Dreams, E.T., Jewel of the Nile,* and *Dances with Wolves.*

New Agers see great spirituality in Indian medicine men, Hindu gurus, Tibetan lamas, Sufi mystics, Zen teachers, and Oriental hermits. They are united in their rejection of the God of the Bible, the deity of Christ, and the personality of the Holy Spirit. Jesus is repackaged as the cosmic Christ. In a do-it-yourself religion, we ought not be surprised to find a make-your-own Jesus!

Desperately seeking answers to the great human problems of our time, the New Ager turns to himself, the planet, the forces of nature, and the spirit world for help. But in his quest, he misses the true Christ—the real source of the peace, security, and stability he seeks.

In the meantime, New Agers are left hoping for some great cosmic deliverer to rescue the world and preserve its peace. Constance Cumbey is right when she says, "For the first time in history there is a viable movement—the New Age movement—that truly meets all the scriptural requirements for the antichrist and the political movement that will bring him on the world scene."[18]

The stage has certainly been set for a new world order based upon a subjective view of reality. It will only be a matter of time until the objective standards of truth will be totally eroded in the modern world. We are getting closer, and the only real question left is: How much time do we have until it's too late?

Globalism and the World Economy

No one could buy or sell unless he had the mark, which is the name of the beast or the number of his name.
—Revelation 13:17

Times are changing more rapidly than ever before. So vast and sweeping are these changes that John Naisbitt calls them "Megatrends."[1] These trends of the times impact the whole globe simultaneously. No longer can single nations pretend to exist only in their little corner of the world. To the contrary, we are fast becoming a global village.

Robert Reich of Harvard University recently stated: "We are living through a transformation that will rearrange the politics and economics of the coming century. . . . Each nation's primary political task will be to cope with the centrifugal forces of the global economy."[2] Reich sees the coming global economy as an inevitable force that will virtually sweep nationalism away. The value of a given society or an individual worker will be his ability to contribute to the world economy.

During the nineteenth century, closely knit networks of local economies were transformed into national economies. Today the national economies are being transformed into a global one. Initially, America led the way toward a global economy modeled on American capitalism. Today the New Europe is leading the way to a system that is often viewed as capable of setting the economic standards for the whole world.

Such ideas as "buy American" are becoming less of a reality all the time. Reich notes that when an American buys a Pontiac from General Motors, he or she "engages unwittingly in an international transaction." Of $20,000 paid to GM, approximately $5,600 goes to South Korea for routine labor; $3,500 goes to Japan for advanced components; $1,500 to West Germany for styling and design engineering; $800 to Taiwan, Singapore, and Japan for small electronic components; $500 to Britain for advertising and marketing services; and about $100 to Ireland and Barbados for data processing. The balance of $8,000 goes to manufacturers in Detroit, bankers and lawyers in Washington, and General Motors stockholders.[3]

This is a typical example of how the "global web" already works. In time, it will become even more complex, touching virtually every industry in America. The interrelations of multinational corporations and the international cooperation of corporations within different nations are not only the trend of the future—it is here now.

Caught in the Global Web

Gilbert Williamson, president of NCR Corporation, recently said, "We at NCR think of ourselves as a globally competitive company that happens to be headquartered in the United States."[4] Like many American products, American corporations are becoming more and more internationalized. They are fast becoming part of the global web in which much of what they buy and sell comes from other countries.

For example, 40 percent of IBM's world employees are non-Americans. Robert Reich notes that IBM Japan employs 18,000 Japanese workers, and with annual sales of $6 billion, it is one of Japan's leading exporters of computers.[5] The question is whether it is an American or Japanese company—or both!

Whirlpool is in an even more complex situation. It recently cut its American work force by 10 percent, shifted production to Mexico, bought Dutch-owned Phillips appliances, and employs 43,500 people in 45 countries. Is it an American company because it has American headquarters or because the majority of its stockholders are Americans? Or is it an international company that happens to be headquartered in America?

Who Will Lead the Way?

No country is better positioned to lead the way in the economic boom of the twenty-first century than the United States. John Naisbitt writes:

> In the global economic competition of the information economy, the quality and innovativeness of human resources will spell the difference. In this

regard no country in the world is better positioned
than the United States.[6]

Naisbitt and Pat Aburdene go on to predict that well-
educated, skilled information workers will earn the highest
wages in history, further reinforcing an economic boom in
the years ahead. He argues that the further the information economy evolves, the better the economy will do in
the future as the middle class moves upward in its mobility.

In the meantime, the European Union is trying to catch
up to the United States and Japan. Naisbitt and Aburdene
note that the changes in Europe are economically driven
as a response to the global competition. "Politics is not driving the change," they observe "but being pulled by it."[7]

The philosophy behind the New Europe is to forge one
cohesive market in order to compete on a global scale. In
order for this to become a reality, physical barriers, such as
customs posts and border controls, will have to be
removed. Technical barriers involving different standards
and regulations will have to be unified. And, fiscal barriers,
such as taxes, will have to be standardized. When the
process is complete, it will mean:

- A Greek lawyer could set up a practice in
  Barcelona, and a Spanish shoe company could
  open a shop in Ireland.

- American businesspeople will be able to fly to
  Europe, pass through customs once, and visit
  11 other member countries.

- A British bank could be a partner in the Paris
  fashion industry.

All in all, this means there will be more competition at
all levels of the single market, bringing a greater choice of

goods and services at better prices. For most Europeans this will be a tremendous step forward economically. The high-speed computer network across Europe will bring the continent together in a manner no military or political action could ever hope to do. Thus, the political unification of Europe will ride on the shoulders of the economy.

Is Prophecy Being Fulfilled?

Evangelicals view the changes in Europe with some concern. While economic cooperation could make for more peaceful relations among the European members, it also seems to link together the basic units of the old Roman Empire. Biblical prophecy warns that in the end times, ten nations will emerge out of the old Roman Empire and control Europe politically and economically. Eventually, the Antichrist himself will gain control of that conglomerate and attempt to rule the whole world.

Daniel 2:31-35 predicts such a development in the prophecy of the great image, in which the two legs represent the East (Greek) and West (Latin) divisions of the Roman Empire and the ten toes represent the kingdom of the Antichrist. Revelation 13:17 warns of a coming world ruler, "the beast," who controls the world economy: "No one could buy or sell unless he had the mark, which is the name of the beast or the number of his name."

There is certainly nothing morally wrong with computers, televisions, satellites, and cashless financial transactions. But many Christians are concerned where all this might lead. It appears that we are slowly but surely becoming the victims of our own technological advancements. We are being swept down the corridor of time to an ominous date with destiny. We are steadily moving toward the inevitable globalization of our planet. National identities and interests will continue to be submerged by a global worldview. In time, America could find herself swept along the tide with everyone else.

Instead of resting on our laurels, America needs a spiritual revival and a reawakening of a vision for world leadership. We cannot expect the world to follow us if we are not leading the way.

Materialism vs. Spirituality

The great problem with materialism is that it also elevates an aspect of the creation to the level of idolatry. It is the worship of the almighty dollar that replaces the Almighty God. It is the belief that money and possessions will fill the spiritual void and bring meaning and purpose to one's life. In an age of selfism, issues like the selfish pursuit of money, power, and influence are everyday occurrences. Television shows and movies feed the greedy desires of people, leaving little or no room for the pursuit of the spiritual values of life.

Pat Robertson is correct when he says, "The power to create money and to regulate its quantity is the power to control the life of a nation."[8] He goes on to note that when a nation gives the control of its money to an outside source, it has surrendered the control of its future to that outside authority. This is the very issue that cost Margaret Thatcher her job as British Prime Minister. Linking the British pound to the European Community's Currency Unit (ECU) would in essence place Britain's economy under the control of the president of the European Community. Thatcher fought this idea, but John Major accepted it.

Today, Britain is helping lead the way into the future for the European Union (EU).

Robertson argues that if the power to create and regulate money is taken away from the president and the Congress of the United States, the American people will also effectively lose democratic control of their own destiny. We in the United States dare not allow ourselves to be drawn into a global money system that is controlled by powers outside the United States, but every pressure will be brought to bear on us to do so.

In the meantime, spiraling national debt is rising out of control. The entire global economy perilously survives from year to year, controlled by large central banking systems. Continued merger of these systems will eventually, in effect, create a one-world economy controlled by a handful of powerful people.

The idea of a world superstate empowered by a world economy is fast becoming a reality. Whether it takes 10 years or 100 years to formulate, such a system is beginning to emerge. Globalists are already promoting the ideas of transnational corporations, universal credit systems, and a world currency controlled by a world bank. In light of this, we have every reason to ask: Can the rise of the Antichrist be right around the corner?

False Religion and the New World Order

The greatest conflict of our times will not be fought on a battlefield between nations. It will be fought in heavenly places between the forces of God and Satan. The spiritual conflict of our times is but an extension of the spiritual conflict that has always existed. The deceptions of Satan may appear to change from time to time, but they really remain basically the same: the lust of the eyes, the lust of the flesh, and the pride of life.

Herbert Schlossberg has correctly observed that the personification of these deceptions is idolatry. He writes, "Idolatry in its larger meaning is properly understood as any substitution of what is created for the creator."[9] He goes on to note that Western society, in turning away from Christianity, has turned to materialism and to nature itself ("save the planet") as the two great idols of our time. Yet he adds, "The technological flowering and economic expansion of the twentieth century has been accompanied by an astonishing growth in pessimism, even despair."[10]

The Bible not only predicts the rise of a false messiah (Antichrist) over the world economy, but it also predicts the coming of a false prophet over the world religious system (Revelation 13:11; 19:20). Who he is or when he will arise is a matter of speculation. Medieval Christians viewed Mohammed as the False Prophet. Protestant Reformers saw the Catholic pope as the Antichrist. More recent identifications have been suggested as well, including: Bill Clinton, Billy Graham, Henry Kissinger, Boris Yeltsin, and Ronald Reagan.

While it may be too soon too guess the identity of the Antichrist, one thing is certain—the cry for religious ecumenism (unity) is growing louder all the time. Some have gone so far as to try to label Hindus, Buddhists, and Muslims as fellow believers. But there is a vast difference between the uniqueness of Jesus Christ and the so-called spirituality of other religions. All other religions teach that man must (by some means) work his way to God. Christianity teaches that God has worked His way to us by sending His Son to die for our sins. All other religions teach "try harder." Christianity teaches, "Give up! And trust God to take care of your spiritual destiny."

When Jesus said "I am the way and the truth and the life. No one comes to the Father except through me" (John 14:6), He was making his most narrow and dogmatic statement of all. He was proclaiming His uniqueness in the plan of divine salvation. This claim and our Lord's great commission to evangelize the entire world stand in opposition to all other religious claims. They set Christianity apart from the other world religions because Christianity is based on *faith in what Christ did*, not faith in what we can do.

We must come to the end of ourselves in order to cast ourselves totally upon God's grace for our salvation. God has made provision for our sins in the sacrifice of His own Son; Jesus' death on the cross was one of substitution. He took our place and died vicariously for our sins. He also rose from the dead to triumph over sin and death, and He offers everlasting life to all who would receive Him by faith.

Ecumenical attempts to ally Christianity with non-Christian religions truly nullifies the unique evangelistic appeal of the church. Once we drop our own beliefs, we have nothing to offer to an unbelieving world. The uniqueness of Christianity *is* Christ! He is the *only* incarnate Son of God to die for the sins of the world and to rise again from the dead; therefore, we ought to proclaim his uniqueness as the *only* Savior of sinners!

The only real hope to turn our generation away from the mindless pursuit of materialism is to call it back to the spiritual values that give real meaning and purpose to life. That is what Jesus meant when He said, "Seek first his kingdom and his righteousness, and all these things will be given to you as well" (Matthew 6:33).

Apostasy and Deception

The Bible (2 Thessalonians 2:3) warns us that before the Antichrist rises to power, there first will be a "falling away" (Greek, *apostasia*). Most commentators take this to be a warning that in the last days many will depart from the Christian faith. Warnings like this appear throughout the New Testament: "In later times some will abandon the faith" (1 Timothy 4:1). "In the last times there will be scoffers who will follow their own ungodly desires" (Jude 18). "In the last days scoffers will come, scoffing and following their own evil desires. They will say, 'Where is this "coming" he promised?' " (2 Peter 3:3,4).

Such *warnings* run throughout the New Testament. Each challenges the present generation of believers to hold fast to the truth and warns of the dangers of capitulating to unbelief. In our Lord's letters in the Revelation to the seven churches, He often referred to false doctrine as something He hated (Revelation 2:15 KJV). Such hatred is not mere intellectual hatred of a wrongly conceived idea, but a deep-seated hatred of errors that corrupt the truth and pull people away from Him.

These are the warnings of a God whose Word is to be taken seriously. They represent the very nature and character of God. They also express His will and purpose for this world. You see, there is more at stake in the issue of globalism than individualism or nationalism. The ultimate question is: Whose world is this? Is it God's world or is it man's world?

This is the very point where Evangelical Christians part company with globalists, New Agers, planetarians, and others who elevate the planet to the place of God. We believe the real, infinite, personal God has a plan for *His* planet. We also believe Christians are to share in that plan.

Even the Old Testament prophets saw beyond the borders of Israel to proclaim God's universal plan for the whole world. "[I will] gather all nations and tongues, and they will come and see my glory" (Isaiah 66:18). "But the LORD rises upon you and his glory appears over you. Nations will come to your light" (Isaiah 60:2,3). "The wilderness will rejoice and blossom. . . . It will burst into bloom. . . . They will see the glory of the LORD" (Isaiah 35:1,2). "Israel will bud and blossom and fill all the world with fruit" (Isaiah 27:6). "In the last days the mountain of the LORD's temple will be established . . . and all nations will stream to it" (Isaiah 2:2).

In the New Testament, we are clearly commanded to take the gospel to the entire world. Jesus said: "Therefore go and make disciples of all nations, baptizing them in the name of the Father and of the Son and of the Holy Spirit" (Matthew 28:19). He also promised: "But you will receive power when the Holy Spirit comes on you; and you will be my witnesses in Jerusalem, and in all Judea and Samaria, and to the ends of the earth" (Acts 1:8).

Our Lord paralleled the *worldwide preaching of the gospel* with the timing of His second coming. He said: "And this gospel of the kingdom will be preached in the whole world as a testimony to all nations, and then the end will come" (Matthew 24:14). No date is given to calculate *when* this will be fulfilled, but the promise of Scripture is clear. When the last convert to come to faith in Christ completes the body of Christ, the Church Age will conclude, and Christ will return to rapture the church to heaven.

Since we do not know when that process will be complete, we must be faithful to preach the gospel to all people everywhere. We can only guess how many nations are left to hear the good news, but the rapid spread of the gospel by radio, television, and satellite must be hurling us toward the end of history faster than ever before.

God's Plan for the World

The Bible emphasizes the fact that God has a plan for the entire world. His plan includes the people of earth as well as the planet Earth. The whole earth is pictured as His domain (Isaiah 66:1). It is the place He created (Genesis 1:1) and where He intervenes in the affairs of man (Ephesians 1:9,10; Romans 6:8-21). It is the place to which Christ came (Hebrews 10:5) and where He lived, died, and rose again (Luke 2:11,12; 23:50-53; 24:1-6). It is also the place to which He promised one day to return (John 14:2,3; Acts 1:11).

The earth is also pictured in Scripture as the place of the last great conflict of mankind. It is God's world, but it is also inhabited by sinful people who pollute, destroy, and defile it. Therefore, the earth will suffer terrible cataclysmic disasters in the last days. Revelation 8:7–9:21 describes air pollution, water pollution, deforestation, and the annihilation of over half the earth's population. The prophets described this time as the wrath of the Lord (Isaiah 13:13), the harvest of judgment (see Micah 4:11,12), and the grapes of wrath (see Isaiah 5:1-7). The book of Revelation calls its final phase the "battle of Armageddon" (16:16).

Despite the coming global holocaust, the Bible reminds us this will not yet be the end of the earth. "If those days had not been cut short," Jesus said, "no one would survive" (Matthew 24:22). Christ's return will come just in time to spare the world. The prophet Zechariah tells us that the survivors of this great battle will go up to Jerusalem year after year to "worship the King, the Lord Almighty" (Zechariah 14:16).

Premillennialists believe that Jesus Christ will reign on the earth from Jerusalem for 1,000 years (Revelation 20:1-6). We believe this millennial kingdom will be a literal kingdom on the earth because that's what the Bible promises (see Revelation 5:10). The 1,000-year reign of Christ will be marked by unparalleled peace and prosperity on earth.

Only after the millennium of Christ's rule will the earth finally be destroyed by fire (Revelation 20:7-9; 2 Peter 3:10-12). Or, as the King James Version puts it, "elements will melt with fervent heat" (2 Peter 3:10). After this, the Bible points to a new heaven and a new earth as the home of the righteous (see 2 Peter 3:13; Revelation 21–22). The earth is not our final destiny. We are just pilgrims passing through this vale of tears. Our real destiny is our eternal home in heaven. Yet this does not mean we should be careless with our mandate to care for the earth. It is still our Father's world, and as the hymnwriter put it: "Though the wrong seems oft so strong, God is the Ruler yet."

Man may conceive new world orders or global economies or international systems, but the only world order destined to survive for eternity will be the kingdom of God. The Bible resounds with this great promise: "The kingdom of the world has become the kingdom of our Lord and of his Christ, and he will reign forever and ever" (Revelation 11:15).

Future Political Super-State

*And I saw a beast coming up out of
the sea.*

—Revelation 13:1

The future design of the European Union will lead to economic, monetary, and political unity in the near future. "The vision of a 'United States of Europe' set out in Winston Churchill's famous speech at Zurich in 1946 remains our objective in the process of European unification," announced Helmut Kohl of Germany in *The European,* Europe's first national newspaper.[1] Using the reunification of Germany as his model, Chancellor Kohl urged the peoples of Europe to move ahead as quickly as possible.

On February 7, 1992, the 12 nations of the European Community signed a unity treaty paving the way for the fulfillment of the full political union of Europe.[2] The signing of the European Union Treaty lays the foundation for a European federation that could one day rival the economic and political influence of the United States.

The modern European Union began when six nations signed the Treaty of Rome in 1957. These six were: Belgium, Germany, Luxembourg, France, Italy, and the Netherlands—with a combined population over 220 million people. In 1973, Denmark, Ireland, and Great Britain joined what was then called the European Economic Community (EEC), bringing 66 million more people into what would become the European Union (EU). In 1981, Greece joined the EEC. In 1986, Portugal and Spain were added. Less than 30 years after the signing of the Treaty of Rome in 1957, the New Europe was 336 million strong. In 1995, Austria, Finland, and Sweden joined the EU, bringing the total population to 362 million in 15 member nations.

The Point of No Return

"We have now passed the point of no return," announced Dutch Prime Minister Ruud Lubbers when the document was signed.[3] Despite earlier restraint, even the British are showing excitement about the New Europe. British Foreign Secretary Douglas Hurd said: "This is a good treaty for Britain and for Europe." Portugal's Prime Minister Anibal Silva called the treaty a "wise balance between ambition and prudence, idealism and pragmatism."

The significance of the new Union Treaty is that it sets in motion Europe's desire to increase its international political force in proportion to its growing economic clout. It also sets in motion plans for monetary union, including a central bank and a single European currency. No matter how it shapes up, the future means a New Europe.

Helmut Kohl views this transition with great optimism. He writes, "Love of freedom and respect for the dignity and rights of neighbors is the cornerstone of a future Pan-European order of peace, in which all peoples live together in liberty."[4]

Going even further, Germany's foreign minister Hans-Dietrich Genscher states: "The mentality of the nation-state has been consigned to the past."[5] He adds that Europe "must contribute to a New World Order which focuses on the individual, his dignity and inalienable rights." Genscher further adds: "We want to strengthen the United Nations. We want a New World Order in which the human rights covenants of the United Nations will ensure protection for civil rights equality with economic and social rights."

The mind-set of Europe now seems to be cast in cement. Europeans are moving toward economic, political, and military unity, ultimately under the banner of the United Nations. While secularists see this as a renewed hope for international peace and cooperation, many Evangelicals view it with great concern. The super global state seems to be just around the corner.

Where Is It All Headed?

Ours may not be exactly the world envisioned by George Orwell or Aldous Huxley, but it is certainly a mix of the two. Somewhere between the Big Brother of Orwell's *1984* and the world gone mad on materialism in a value-emptied culture of high technology in Huxley's *Brave New World*, we find the current tension in our world today. Malachi Martin, a former Vatican professor, calls it the great "Millennial Endgame."[6] He predicts a final confrontation between the secularists, socialists, and the church for the new global hegemony which is now upon us. "The competition is about who will establish the first one-world system government that has ever existed in the society of nations," Martin writes.[7]

These are not just the sentiments of a few speculators. Everyone is talking about the possibility of a new world order. Former President George Bush spoke frequently about this concept. Ever since *Time* magazine (December 11, 1989) flashed the headline, "Building a New World Order," the idea has been a hot topic among Christians and secularists alike.[8]

With the collapse of the Soviet empire, the unification of Germany, and talk of a United States of Europe, we are certainly on the threshold of a new day of international politics. Many people are predicting an unprecedented wave of worldwide democracy and capitalism. Still others, like Larry Burkett, are predicting an economic disaster.[9]

The wheels of rapid change are certainly spinning across Europe these days. "Europhoria" is the mood of exuberance that has captured the spirit of cooperation within the European Community. The unification in 1992 by the 12 members of the EEC created the largest trading bloc and free-market economy in the world today.

Time magazine declared: "Project 1992 has given fresh momentum . . . to taking Western Europe further down the road to unity."[10] *U.S. News & World Report* predicted a unified Western Europe by 2000.[11] We are virtually there. Europe has the potential, for the first time in a millennium–and-a-half to become a unified power—the political super-state of the future.

Can East Meet West?

The great issue facing the attempt to build a New Europe is whether the Eastern bloc countries can become full participants with the Western bloc. This will not be an easy process. Old hatreds, fears, and jealousies divide Europe into a patchwork quilt of ethnic rivals and bitter enemies. But let us suppose that the newly united Germany and Russia are able to lead the way in that unification. The end result would be the largest and most powerful nation on earth—a Europe that stretches from the Atlantic to the Pacific!

The world has obviously come to a great crossroads today. On the one hand, peaceful cooperation seems to be the spirit of the times. Everyone is talking democracy, capitalism, peace, and prosperity. For Europe, the future looks brighter than it has since the days of the Roman Empire. On the other hand, the seeds of world destruction may well have been sown to such a degree that there is no retreat from disaster.

The decisions we make today will determine the course of action we take in the years ahead. As Evangelical Christians, we need to remind the world of its great spiritual needs. The spiritual emptiness of atheistic communism has left the people of Europe in a vacuum of value-emptied secularism. No matter how hard they try to experiment with freedom, democracy, and free-market enterprise, they cannot build a great society without God. If the democratization of Eastern Europe results in nothing more than empty materialism without God, we have truly failed to set it free from the worst kind of tyranny. Only when they discover Christian beliefs, values, and principles can they hope to be very successful.

Europe is at the crossroads. Which way she goes in the future may well depend on what we do today to make Christ and His church known there. Without Him there is no real hope for the future; with Him there could yet be time for spiritual revival on the continent that has so often forgotten God.

Europe Beyond 2000

Arno Froese, executive director of *Midnight Call Ministries,* himself a European by background, believes the coming European powerhouse will produce the empire of the Antichrist. He writes, "Not capitalism, or communism, but social-capital democracy is becoming the driving force which will supersede all others."[12] Froese adds, "The phenomenal growth of Europe is based strictly on economy and finance at this point in time."[13]

European economic strategists project the European Central Bank (ECB) will control the new currency by the year 2000.[14] Shortly thereafter the euro dollar will become the dominant world currency. In the meantime, Froese explains that we already have a world currency in the form of credit cards. He notes: "When you take your credit card and travel to any part of the world, you can instantaneously buy virtually anything in any currency.... We don't have to wait for a one world financial system to appear because it is already working right now at this moment! The world already functions as a global community."[15]

In his controversial but insightful book *How Democracy Will Elect the Antichrist,* Arno Froese correctly emphasizes the relationship of the Antichrist to the New Europe. He writes, "One of the most difficult things to grasp for citizens who have lived under a free system, such as democracy, is the fact that it will usher in the new age of the Antichrist—a temporary time of peace and prosperity."[16]

One of the great ironies of history will be the fact that the most successful human system ever devised will be used by Satan to bring the world dictator to power. While this may sound incredible to some, recall that Adolph Hitler was originally chosen by the German people in a democratic election. Once elected to power, dictators quickly eliminate further elections and maintain power by force.

Froese astutely observes: "The new European power structure will fulfill the prophetic predictions which tell us that a one world system will be implemented. When established, it will fall into the hands of . . . the Antichrist."[17] What we are now witnessing in Europe are the initial steps leading to the global system of the last days.

Why Europe?

Much has been written about the empire of the Antichrist. Some believe it will be centered in Babylon (Iraq). Others have suggested America as a possibility. But the Bible itself clearly identifies Europe as the location of the final phase of Gentile world power. Americans are quick to ask: "Where is the United States in biblical prophecy?" But the better question is: "Where is Europe in biblical prophecy?"

The United States (USA) did not exist when the Bible was written. Therefore, it does not clearly appear in the prophetic Scriptures. One can only make a case for America in prophecy by associating it with Europe. As a nation of predominantly European transplants, the United States could possibly qualify as the "young lions" of Tarshish (Ezekiel 38:13 KJV). The U.S. also could be included with general references to the revived Roman Empire. Otherwise, prophecy students have to stretch a great deal to find the U.S. in the biblical text.

Israel is the center of all biblical prophecy. She is also the "land bridge" between Europe, Asia, and Africa. Therefore, biblical history—as well as biblical prophecy—is focused on Israel and her relationship to those nations that played a role in the Old Testament record.

Daniel's series of visions for the nations were given to him in regard to their relationship to Israel. He was taken captive to ancient Babylon by King Nebuchadnezzar in 605 B.C. While still a student in training, Daniel interpreted the king's dream about the great statue with a head of gold, arms of silver, belly of brass, legs of iron, and feet of iron and clay. According to the dream, the statue was obliterated by a great rock that filled the whole earth (Daniel 2:31-35).

As he stood before the great Nebuchadnezzar, Daniel told the king that God had revealed "what will happen in days to come" (Daniel 2:27,28). Daniel proceeded to tell Nebuchadnezzar that the king was the head of gold and that after him would arise three other kingdoms inferior to his own. Out of the fourth kingdom would come the ten toes, "partly strong and partly brittle" (Daniel 2:42). "In the time of those kings," Daniel explained, "the God of heaven will set up a kingdom that will never be destroyed. . . . It will itself endure forever" (Daniel 2:44). Notice that the supernatural rock, cut out without hands, struck the ten toes of the statue.

About 50 years later, in 553 B.C. Daniel himself had a vision in which he saw "four great beasts" come up from the sea (Daniel 7). These beasts represented the same four great empires Nebuchadnezzar saw in his dream. What Nebuchadnezzar saw as a beautiful statue, Daniel saw as wild animals about to tear each other apart. He saw a winged lion, which symbolized Babylon. Next came a lopsided bear, stronger on one side than the other. He later identified this second kingdom as Media and Persia (Daniel 8:20). The two arms of the statue and the lopsided appearance of the bear aptly described the dual empire that would eventually be dominated by Persia. Next, he saw a four-winged leopard, which he later identified as Greece (Daniel 8:21). Finally, he saw a fourth beast with ten horns (Daniel 7:7). Its teeth were

Five Kingdoms

Gold   BABYLON

Winged Lion

Silver   MEDIA-PERSIA

Lopsided Bear

Brass   GREECE

4-Winged Leopard

Iron   ROME

10-Horned Monster with Iron Teeth

Iron & clay   KINGDOM OF ANTICHRIST

Little Horn

iron, the same metal as the fourth kingdom in the statue, and it subdued "whatever was left."

The Final Empire

Although the fourth beast is never identified by Daniel, it is clearly Rome, the empire that succeeded Greece. The statue's two legs (Daniel 2:33) seem to indicate the division of Rome into East (Greek-speaking Constantinople) and West (Latin-speaking Rome). The ten horns of this beast parallel the ten toes of the statue (Daniel 2:39-43). They are identified as "ten kings who will come from this kingdom" (Daniel 7:24), after whom will arise "another king," an eleventh king, who will blaspheme God and persecute the saints. Many Bible scholars believe this person is the Antichrist.

Evangelical Christian scholars generally interpret the ten horns of Daniel's fourth beast and the ten toes of the statue as being synonymous. Both grow out of the fourth empire and represent the final phase of it. Premillennialists see a gap of time, the Church Age, separating the legs and the toes, with the stone falling at the *second* coming of Christ, during the final stage of Gentile history.

In Nebuchadnezzer's vision, the stone fell on the ten toes and obliterated the statue to dust, the wind blew the dust away, and the stone filled the whole earth. Premillennialists argue that this has not yet happened. They believe this is a prophetic picture of Christ's return to set up His kingdom on earth at the beginning of the millennium (His 1,000-year reign).

In the meantime, attempts to identify the ten kings pictured by the toes and horns have proven futile. Daniel's vision of the four beasts clearly dates them at the end of time. The "little" horn that rises out of the ten horns (Daniel 7:7,8) is said to continue for "a time (one), times (two) and half a time" (Daniel 7:25), or three-and-one-half times. This is the same time given for the persecution of the "woman" by the beast in the apocalypse (Revelation 12:14; 13:5). This is generally seen to be the three-and-one-half years or 42 months of the great tribulation (the last half of the seven-year tribulation period).

Daniel's prophecies clearly indicate the dominance of Israel by the Gentiles until the time of the Antichrist. Since Rome (legs) and the revived Rome (toes) of the last days are indicated by Daniel's prophecies, Daniel clearly points to Europe/Rome as the final Gentile power. Whether the final form of the fourth kingdom (toes) includes America we can only guess.

When Will This Happen?

Daniel's prophecy of the 70 weeks (Daniel 9) tells us that God put Israel's future on a time clock. God told Daniel that "seventy 'sevens' ['weeks,' KJV] are decreed for your people [Israel] and your holy city [Jerusalem] to finish transgression, to put an end to sin, to atone for wickedness, to bring in everlasting righteousness, to seal up vision and prophecy and to anoint the most holy" (Daniel 9:24).

The prophecy goes on to predict that 7 "sevens" will pass as Jerusalem is rebuilt and 62 more "sevens" will pass, for a total of 69, until the Anointed One (Messiah) will be cut off. This leaves one "seven" left for the future. Bible scholars generally interpret these "sevens" (Hebrew, *shabua)* to refer to units of 7 years; thus, 70 sevens would equal 490 years. By means of simple calculation we can determine that the span of time from Artaxerxes' decree for Nehemiah to rebuild Jerusalem to when the Messiah would be cut off (crucified) is 483 years (69 "sevens"). That would bring us to A.D. 32 on the Jewish calendar, which was the year of Christ's crucifixion."[18]

The Jewish calendar was composed of 360 days or 12 months of 30 days. These are the same figures used to calculate that three-and-one-half years are also 42 months or 1,260 days (Revelation 12:6-14). By following the Jewish calendar, scholars have calculated the beginning date of the Persian Emperor Artaxerxes' decree to send Nehemiah to rebuild the city of Jerusalem (Nehemiah 2:1-9) as Nisan 1 (Jewish calendar) or March 14, 445 B.C. The terminal date would be Nisan 10 (Jewish calendar) or April 6, A.D. 32.

The interval between the decree of Artaxerxes and the triumphal entry of Christ at Jerusalem includes exactly 173,880 days (or 7 x 69 prophetic years of 360 days each). Reckoning the days inclusively according to Jewish practice, Sir Robert Anderson was the first person to work out this computation, and it has been followed by most premillennial scholars.[19] According to Anderson, the 69 weeks of 7 years (483 years) ended on the Sunday of our Lord's triumphal entry into Jerusalem. That initiated His final rejection by the Jews, which led to His crucifixion.

Daniel's Seventieth Week

This leaves one "week" or unit of seven years yet to come. Many premillennialists locate this final seven years in the tribulation period, which will come after the rapture of the church. During these final seven years, God's prophetic clock for Israel will begin to tick again.

Notice that the prophecy of the "seventy sevens" was given to Daniel in regard to his people (the Jews) and their holy city (Jerusalem). All of the 490 years have to do with *Israel*, not the church. This focuses our attention on the fact that Israel plays a prominent role in the tribulation period.

In the meantime, Daniel was told that "war will continue until the end" (Daniel 9:26). That's what Jesus said in the Olivet Discourse (Matthew 24:6). Thus, we can conclude that the "times of the Gentiles" will be marked by wars and by the rise and fall of the four major empires presented in Daniel chapters 2 and 7.

Then Daniel was told of a ruler (prince, KJV) who was yet to come and "destroy the city and the sanctuary" (Daniel 9:26). This ruler will make a covenant (peace treaty) with Israel, then break it in the middle of the seventieth "seven" and turn against Jerusalem and cause "abomination" and "desolation" (Daniel 9:27), which Jesus also referred to in His prophetic message (Matthew 24:15).

The Abomination of Desolation

After Daniel's time, the Jews returned to Jerusalem and reconstructed the temple under Zerubbabel and rebuilt the city walls under Nehemiah. Then the Old Testament revelation closed. For nearly 400 silent years there was no new revelation from God. Malachi had predicted Elijah would come again to turn people's hearts back to God (Malachi 4:5,6). And several prophets had pointed to the coming of the Anointed One (Messiah). But as the Old Testament closes, we are left waiting for these promises to be fulfilled.

During the intertestamental period (the silent years), the Jews were severely persecuted by the Selucid ruler Antiochus IV Epiphanes. In 168 B.C., he vented his wrath on the Jews, as predicted by Daniel, and desecrated the temple (Daniel 11:21-35). (According to historians, this desecration included offering a pig on the holy altar.) Certainly this was an abomination to the Jews (Daniel 11:31), but notice that it happened *before* the Messiah ever arrived. Soon afterward, the Jews revolted under the leadership of Judas Maccabeaus, whose family fought Antiochus' army from 168 to 165 B.C. Their exploits are recorded in the apocryphal books of 1 and 2 Maccabees. After three years of fighting, the Jews were able to restore worship in Jerusalem, and they cleansed the temple with a great Feast of Dedication (Hanukkah) on December 25, 165 B.C.

Eventually the Romans conquered Jerusalem and installed Herod the Great as a puppet king under their authority. In an attempt to appease the Jews, Herod had the temple remodeled and greatly expanded. The initial work took about ten years, but construction continued from 20 B.C. to A.D. 64. The edifice was a magnificent sight. Jesus' own disciples were so impressed with it that they called Jesus' attention to the building. But our Lord shocked them when He predicted that the temple would be destroyed, and not one stone of it would be left standing (Matthew 24:1,2).

When the Jews revolted against Rome in A.D. 66, the angry Romans decided to retaliate by destroying the temple and burning Jerusalem to the ground. The devastation was carried out in A.D. 70 by Titus, the son of Emperor Vespasian. Jerusalem's occupants were either slaughtered or enslaved. A subsequent revolt in A.D. 135, led by Jesus Bar Kochba, a Jewish zealot, also failed. Hadrian, who was Rome's emperor at the time, had the rubble of Jerusalem plowed under, and he erected a Roman city, Aelia Capitolina, from which all

Jews were banned. Certainly this was another abomination and desolation.

Over the centuries that followed, either the Romans, the Arabs, or the Crusaders held Jerusalem. The temple was never rebuilt, and the Jews were scattered in the Great Dispersion (*Diaspora*). Yet Daniel's prophecy looks all the way down the corridor of time until the end. He tells us there is one great "abomination of desolation" still to come.

The Great Tribulation

As Jesus looked down the corridor of time to the end of the present age—an age that would be launched by the preaching of the gospel message and by the empowerment of His disciples with the Holy Spirit—He warned of a time of great tribulation or great distress that would come upon the whole world (Matthew 24:15-28). The "abomination of desolation" (Matthew 24:15 KJV) refers to when Antiochus Epiphanes profaned Jewish temple worship during the intertestamental period (Daniel 9:27; 11:31; 12:11), foreshadowing an even more serious abomination that would occur in the future. Whereas Antiochus offered an unclean pig on the sacred altar of the temple, the Antichrist will offer himself (2 Thessalonians 2:4).

The act of desecration that Daniel had predicted about Antiochus, a pagan Hellenistic ruler, will be repeated even more seriously in the future. This will signal the beginning of the great tribulation on earth. Note that Jesus saw this as a future event, so this abomination is not limited to the past actions of Antiochus. Nor was the abomination fulfilled in the Roman destruction of Jerusalem in A.D. 70, since our Lord tied it to the "great tribulation" (KJV) that is "unequaled from the beginning of the world until now—

and never to be equaled again" (Matthew 24:21). Our Lord went on to explain that the devastation of the great tribulation will be so awful that unless those days were cut short no one would survive (Matthew 24:22).

Jesus further described this coming day of trouble as a time when the sun and moon are darkened and the heavens will be shaken (Matthew 24:29). His description runs parallel to that found in Revelation 16:1-16, where the final hour of the tribulation is depicted by atmospheric darkness, air pollution, and ecological disaster. These cataclysmic events accompany the return of Christ.

Babylon the Great

The book of Revelation speaks at great length in chapters 17–18 about the fall of "Babylon the Great" (Revelation 18:2). This kingdom is personified as "the great whore" (Revelation 17:1 KJV) who has seven heads and ten horns and, according to Revelation 17:5, bears the title "Mystery Babylon."

This woman is described as "drunk with the blood of the saints . . . who bore testimony to Jesus" (Revelation 17:6). The seven heads are "seven hills on which the woman sits" (Revelation 17:9), and the ten horns are the "ten kings" who are yet to come (Revelation 17:12). The woman herself is "the great city that rules over the kings of the earth" (Revelation 17:18). There is little doubt that John is talking about Rome, the great city that ruled the world of his own day and under whose authority he had been banished to the Island of Patmos, where he received the Revelation.

The Babylon mentioned in Revelation 17–18 is the center of the great material, economic, and political system of the last days. It is defined as the source of the world's wealth and prosperity. It is the place where sailors and merchants go to make their fortunes (Revelation 18:11-19). Yet there is a final word of judgment spoken against her: "Fallen! Fallen is Babylon the Great! . . . In one hour your doom has come! . . . All your riches and splendor have vanished. . . . In one hour she has been brought to ruin!" (Revelation 18:2,10,14,19). Whatever this final act of judgment may be, it is instantaneous, devastating, and permanent. The aftermath certainly seems to describe the consequence of a nuclear war. The prophecy tells of people who watch the "smoke of her burning" from their ships, but they will not go near Babylon, perhaps for fear of contamination.

The question often debated among Evangelicals is whether this "Babylon" is the Babylon of ancient times revived in the last days or whether it is symbolic of Rome revived in the last days. Either way, those who view the Revelation as a prophecy of the future must look for a future Babylon or future Rome as the fulfillment of this prediction. In this regard, let us consider several key factors:

1. The early church unanimously viewed Babylon as Rome. None of the early church fathers held that Babylon was to be taken literally. They all viewed it as symbolic of the Roman Empire in general, and the city of Rome in particular.

2. The reformers and puritans were also unanimous in taking Babylon as a symbol of Rome. The only difference was that they extended it to refer to papal Rome as the apostate church of the last days.

3. There is no valid reason today to assume that ancient Babylon will literally be rebuilt and rise to

power overnight as the dominant world city and capital of the Antichrist.

The Babylon of Revelation 17–18 is the greatest city in the whole world. It is portrayed as the capital of the Antichrist, who rules the revived Roman Empire, the final Gentile kingdom. It is a center of commerce, enterprise, and trade. And it is the city that shed the blood of the "martyrs of Jesus." Ancient Babylon does not qualify in any of these regards. Notice the characteristics of *apocalyptical "Babylon"* found in the Revelation:

1. rich and prosperous (17:4)

2. immoral and drunken (17:2)

3. associated with Satan and the beast (17:7,8)

4. city that sits on seven hills (17:9)

5. leader of a ten-nation confederacy with Roman (European) roots (17:10,11)

6. city that rules over many nations (17:15-18)

7. center of commercial enterprise (18:3,11-13)

8. sailors cross the sea to get there (18:17,18)

9. an entertainment capital (18:22,23)

10. burns up in one hour (18:9,10,17-19)

Arno Froese summarizes his own discussion of Mystery Babylon by observing that only Rome qualifies for this identification. He writes, "This city must not only have shed the blood of the martyrs of Jesus, be located on seven hills, and commit political-religious fornication with the leaders of the world, but it must also be seen, when on fire, from the sea. There is no other city on earth that fits the four-fold criteria mentioned. Only Rome qualifies."[20]

The very fact that John calls her identity a mystery ought to be enough to indicate that he does not intend us to take Babylon literally. His subsequent description of this great city makes that point all the more clear. It teaches us to look deeper and see it figuratively rather than literally. Thus, John takes the name of Israel's ancient enemy, Babylon, and uses it for Rome. Adorned in luxury and intoxicated with the blood of the saints, she stands for a dominant world system based on seduction for personal gain over and against the righteous demands of a persecuted minority.

The real tragedy is that she could well include America. While there is no clear prophecy about the United States in the Bible (nor Canada, Australia, South Africa, and so on), it is certainly probable that if a European alliance were to form in fulfillment of these prophecies anytime soon, it would most likely include all the major Western powers. That they could be headed by an American leader is certainly possible, even probable.

Whether apocalyptic Babylon exists today or is still in the process of being formulated, only future generations can judge. What the Bible does make clear is that it has always existed. It is the epitome of the kingdom of Satan— the "city of man." It is opposed to and has always been opposed to the "city of God." It is the blatant expression of the finest efforts of finite minds to rule themselves in opposition to the rule of God. Thus, the greatest and most spectacular of our cities without God are an architectural fist in the face of heaven!

9

War Is
Inevitable!

*Woe! Woe! Woe to the inhabitants of
the earth!*

— Revelation 8:13

In his landmark study, *Power*, Adolf Berle stated,
"Power and love are the oldest known phenomena of
human emotions. Neither wholly yields to rational discussion."[1] He also observed, "Power is a universal experience;
practically every adult has had a measure of it, great or
small, for a brief moment or for an extended time."[2] But he
also warned, "Except in rarest fortune, power leaves men
before their lives are over."

Berle, professor emeritus of law at Columbia University, postulated *five natural laws of power:*[3]

1. Power fills any vacuum in human organization.

2. Power is invariably personal.

3. Power is based on a system of ideas or philosophy.

4. Power is exercised through, and depends on, institutions which limit and control it.

5. Power acts in relation to a field of responsibility.

Berle saw power as the human effort to control chaos. He suggested that in any contest between power and chaos, power would always win. But he also acknowledged that such victories were always temporary in nature until the contest between power and chaos was renewed.

John Kotter has defined power as the measure of a person's potential to get others to do what he or she wants them to do, as well as being able to avoid doing what he or she does not want to do.[4]

Charles Colson has stated, "The history of the last fifty years has validated Nietzsche's argument that man's desire to control his own destiny and to impose his will on others is the most basic human motivation." Nietzsche argued that the "will of power" would eventually fill the vacuum of values in the modern world, and he was right! We are now witnessing the culmination of the deterioration of Western culture. For nearly a century, modern man has been told that he is an animal, and now he is starting to live like one. But like an animal, he has no allegiance to the morals or values of the past. Modern man has struck out on his own, and he is adrift on the sea of relativity.

Aleksandr Solzhenitsyn has said:

> If the world has not approached its end, it has reached a major watershed in history equal in importance to the turn from the Middle Ages to the Renaissance. It will demand from us a spiri-

> tual blaze; we shall have to rise to a new height of
> vision, to a new level of life, where our physical
> nature will not be crushed, as in the Middle Ages,
> but even more importantly, our spiritual being
> will not be trampled upon, as in the Modern Era.[5]

It is this sense of destiny that compels most Evangelicals at the present hour. It is obvious to virtually everyone that what has been viewed as the traditional American culture is in danger of extinction. Whether this threat is real or perceived, it staggers the Evangelical heart with the fear of a secularist future in which God, religion, and religious values have no place.

A godless secular state is the environment necessary to justify war for the common good of the state. As our culture continues to become more secularized, the stage will be set for the justification of war against all who oppose the will of the state. As good a system as democracy is, it can only survive with a moral foundation. Otherwise, a majority of people can legitimatize anything they choose. Just because something is politically correct, doesn't make it morally right.

On the Brink of War

Just prior to the dawn of the new millennium, the Berlin wall was dismantled, Germany was reunited, the Soviet satellites were set free, and the Soviet Union itself became the democratic Commonwealth of Independent states. Unfortunately, when everyone was beginning to believe peace was in sight, Saddam Hussein upset the plans by maliciously invading Kuwait. It wasn't long before headlines read: "Geneva Peace Talks Fail," "War in the Middle East," "U.S. Bombs Baghdad," and "Israel Hit by Missiles."

Satellite broadcasts gave us all front-row seats on the most televised war in modern history.

Prophetic speculation began running at fever pitch. Many were convinced Armageddon was just around the corner. But the United States-led coalition squashed Iraq in one of the most effective wars ever fought. God intervened to give the world a reprieve. What could have been the worst war in modern history was over in a few weeks.

When Saddam Hussein ordered the invasion of Kuwait on August 2, 1990, he unleashed a bloodbath that would eventually claim 100,000 Iraqi lives. What would possess someone to do such a horrible and irrational act? I believe the only legitimate answer is Satan. He is the father of pride, arrogance, extravagance, lies, and murder. The history of our world is sadly dotted with the aftermath of his destructive work in the hearts of people.

The actions of Saddam Hussein remind us of a very real, soon-to-come madman, the Antichrist, who will bring war and destruction to this planet while promising peace and prosperity. It may well be that the hopes and dreams of a new world order will one day smolder in the ashes of a world gone crazy.

The Nuclear Epidemic

A recent article in *U.S. News & World Report* announced: "The West's attempt to prevent the spread of nuclear weapons has failed, and a dangerous new era of nuclear proliferation has begun."[6] The article goes on to report that the collapse of the Soviet system of control and the failure of the Russian economy has unleashed a flood of uranium ore and tons of plutonium on the black market. Much of this is coming from the Muslim Central Asian republics and could well end up equipping Iran, Iraq, or Syria with nuclear warheads in the near future. In addition to the instability of the Middle East, it is now commonly believed North Korea is also on the verge of creating a nuclear bomb, with Japan and Taiwan not far behind.

Stephen Budiansky notes that every country that has ever attempted to build a nuclear bomb has done it by building their own bomb-making complex.[7] The technology already exists and can easily be copied. The real problem for would-be nuclear powers, he says, "is obtaining plutonium or highly enriched uranium to fuel the explosive chain reaction." He further notes that North Korea has developed its own supply from graphite, which exists there in abundance.

By 1987, North Korea had constructed a fully operating nuclear reactor, producing about 20 pounds of plutonium a year—more than enough to equip a nuclear weapon. The technology to go with the raw materials is often provided to countries such as North Korea, Libya, and Algeria by former Soviet technicians for hire.

Fortunately for the present, the Russian government is attempting to control its stockpile of 115 tons of plutonium and 500 tons of highly enriched uranium. But attempts to sell off supplies as reactor fuel for "peaceful purposes" could easily increase the world supply to volatile nations.

Carla Anne Robbins warns: "The breakup of the (Soviet Union) poses the biggest proliferation threat facing the world today."[8] U.S. government officials have already reported "shopping" expeditions to Russia and Kazakhstan by delegations from Iraq, Iran, and Libya. The instability that resulted from the transfer of power from the Soviet Union to the Commonwealth of Independent States often resulted in temporary loss of control at various weapon sites. There is no way to avoid the fact that the instability of the Russian government means uncertainty for the world's future. While the United States has officially expressed confidence in Russia's ability to contain the nuclear weapons and technology, it is also obvious that nuclear scientists could easily be hired on the world market.

I believe God is giving us an open window of His grace. We have an unparalleled opportunity to evangelize the spiritually deprived peoples of Eastern Europe. We must act quickly before that window of opportunity closes. We have no guarantee that the U.S. and Russia will remain on friendly terms indefinitely.

How Close Is Disaster?

Albert Einstein warned that the atomic age would propel the world toward unparalleled catastrophe. In his blockbuster bestseller *The End*, Ed Dobson reminds us that "Hiroshima is a microcosm of what could and might happen.... The current nuclear arsenal has the potential to wipe out civilization as we know it."[9] Scientists now estimate the staggering potential nuclear holocaust that would result from a nuclear war:

Human Toll

- 750 million to 1 billion people killed

- 340 million seriously injured

- 33% of the survivors incapacitated

Environmental Toll

- water contamination

- radiation fallout

- toxic rain

- uncontrollable fires

- inability to grow food[10]

Nuclear war will kill at least one-third of the population of earth and render the environment unsuitable for those who survive. "Everything would change forever," Dobson writes.[11] Futurists Alvin and Heidi Toffler have said, "We appear to be plunging into a new dark age of tribal hate, planetary desolation, and wars multiplied by wars."[12] The world scene is tenuous at best. The Tofflers note there are nearly 200 members of the United Nations, and 60 of them have waged war in the last 50 years. They state, "In fact, in the 2,340 weeks that passed between 1945 and 1990, the earth enjoyed a grand total of only three that were truly war-free."[13]

The Tofflers observe that we have a *trisected global society* with three types of politico-economic systems: 1) agrarian, 2) industrial, 3) informational. These move at various "clock speeds" as they intersect one another. Thus, a crisis in one sector can trigger a response in another, as in the case of Somalia (agrarian) or Iraq (industrial). They write, "Nothing marks today's moment of history . . . more strikingly than the acceleration of change. . . . This acceleration, partly driven by faster communications, means that hot spots can erupt into the global system almost overnight. . . . A 'small' war in a remote place can, through a series of often unpredictable events, snowball into a giant conflagration."[14]

Only a Matter of Time

Nuclear war is inevitable. It is only a matter of time until someone somewhere has nuclear weapons and the capability to deliver them—and is willing to push the button. Initially, it may only be a limited explosion in an isolated place. But human nature being what it is, sooner or later the world will face the reality of a nuclear holocaust.

Dobson notes that biblical prophecies have incredible similarities to a potential nuclear war. He points to Peter's prediction that the world will be destroyed by fire in the last days (2 Peter 3:7-12). Dobson points out three major characteristics of these *cataclysmic events* described by Peter.[15]

1. *Explosion in the heavens:* "The heavens will disappear with a roar" (verse 10).

   The bomb dropped at Hiroshima exploded in the air 500 meters above the city.

2. *Things melting with heat:* "The elements will melt in the heat" (verse 12).

   In a nuclear explosion, one-third of the energy is given off in heat, creating huge fireballs.

3. *Destruction of the earth:* "The earth and everything in it will be laid bare" (verse 10).

   In the aftermath of a nuclear explosion, forests, grasslands, and rivers would be burned and destroyed.

"The book of Revelation predicts similar events at the end of the world," Dobson adds.[16] He notes that the Revelation predicts massive global destruction from "hail and fire" and a "huge mountain, all ablaze." These judgments result in:

> A third of the earth burned.
> A third of the trees burned.
> All the green grass burned.
> The sea turned to blood.

Rivers and waters polluted.
Darkness and air pollution.

Is This Armageddon?

The term *Armageddon* (Greek, *Harmegedon*) appears only once in the entire Bible—in Revelation 16:16. The location, the hill Megiddo, overlooks the Valley of Jezreel in northern Israel. It was the site of numerous biblical conflicts (see Joshua 12:7,12; Judges 5:19; 2 Kings 23:29). Megiddo itself served as a military stronghold for several generations (see Judges 1:27; 2 Kings 9:27). It is in this great valley in Israel's breadbasket that the New Testament places the final conflict between Christ and the Antichrist. Old Testament prophecies also point to a final conflict between Israel and the nations of the world in the last days (see Joel 3:2-14; Zechariah 14:1-5; Zephaniah 3:8).

Theologically, Armageddon is a symbolic term for the final apocalyptic conflict between the forces of Christ and Antichrist. It is not limited to the Valley of Jezreel, but its focus is there. The entire series of battles instigated by the Antichrist will climax at Armageddon when the kings of the earth and the whole world converge for the "battle of that great day of God Almighty" (Revelation 16:14). J. Dwight Pentecost notes that this is not an isolated battle but a military campaign that includes several battles and extends throughout the tribulation period.[17]

Biblical references to the final end-times conflict also refer to events in the Valley of Jehoshaphat (Joel 3:2,12), the Lord's coming from Edom (Isaiah 34:6), and Jerusalem itself being the center of the conflict (see Zechariah 12:2-10; 14:2). While the troops may be deployed from Armageddon, they apparently spread out to cover the land. The conflict extends from the plains of Esdraelon on the north, down through Jerusalem, out into the Valley of Jehoshaphat, and southward to Edom.

The Bible describes the nations of the world, under the leadership of the Antichrist, allied against Israel and the people of God in the last days. Differences of opinion exist among premillennialists regarding the relationship of the battle of Armageddon to the biblical predictions of the invasion of the king of the north and the king of the south (see Daniel 11:4-45). Revelation 16:12 also refers to the drying up of the Euphrates River as a prelude to this great battle. With this miraculous act, the way will be paved for the kings of the east to join the final battle.

Dr. John Walvoord notes that "the Battle of Armageddon will occur during the final days of the Great Tribulation,"[18] after the pouring out of the bowls (vials, KJV) of judgment (see Revelation 16). It will be the culmination of the ongoing conflict between the Antichrist and people of God. Walvoord also notes: "Armies will be fighting in Jerusalem on the very day of the second coming of Christ (Zechariah 14:1-3)."[19] At the point of Christ's return, the battle of Armageddon will be won by Jesus and His triumphant church (bride of Christ), which return with Him (Revelation 19:11-14).

The battle of Armageddon also culminates in the final collapse of political and ecclesiastical Babylon. The kingdom of the Antichrist and its false religious system will be utterly destroyed at the same time (see Revelation 17–18). Again, premillennialists disagree on whether Babylon refers to literal Babylon in modern Iraq or whether it is a symbolic term for Rome. In either case, the Scripture makes it clear that Babylon represents the global political and ecclesiastical system of the end times.

At the battle of Armageddon, Christ is victorious by the power of His spoken word. The Antichrist and the False Prophet are defeated and cast into the lake of fire, and Satan is bound in the abyss (bottomless pit, KJV) for 1,000 years during the millennial reign of Christ on earth (Revelation 19:17–20:3). Thus, the last great war will take place in relation to the second coming of Christ.

Thomas Ice and Timothy Demy note that the battle of Armageddon is "a battle that never really takes place," in the sense of achieving its objectives. The war itself leaves the earth devastated, but the final assault on Christ is aborted. They write, "God will intervene and Jesus Christ will return to rescue His chosen people Israel. The Lord and His angelic army will destroy the armies, capture the Antichrist and the False Prophet, and cast them into the lake of fire."[20]

No rational person wants war; death and destruction are the consequences of a fallen world. They may be inevitable, but their inevitability is certainly no reason to want to hasten Armageddon. It will come soon enough. In the meantime, we should pray for peace and work for peace so that the gospel of Jesus Christ may be preached in all the world.

The Gospel According to Power

Jesus' preaching of the kingdom of God contradicted every prevailing view of religion and politics of His day. He rejected the asceticism and isolationism of the Essenes. He refused to play the games of political accommodation that characterized the Sadducees and Pharisees. He totally confounded the Herodians and refused to give cause to the Zealots (see Matthew 22:15-46). He stood alone with a uniquely new message, emphasizing that the kingdom of God was within the hearts of true believers. Thus, they were free from the suppression of political domination or the corruption of political compromise. They were citizens of heaven as well as earth, and their mission on earth was to make people citizens of the kingdom of God.

Jesus offered the people of His day a whole new way of looking at politics and power. He clearly announced, "My kingdom is not of this world" (John 18:36). Ironically, His own disciples struggled with this issue. At the time of His ascension, they asked, "Lord, are you at this time going to restore the kingdom to Israel?" (Acts 1:6). He reminded them that He had another priority and that was the preaching of the gospel to the whole world (Acts 1:8). By the end of the book of Acts we find the apostle Paul "preaching the kingdom of God" free from all political entanglement (see Acts 28:31).

In time, the very government of Rome that had persecuted Jews and Christians alike became "Christian" under Constantine in the fourth century A.D. One would expect that those who had been so severely persecuted that they were driven into the catacombs would have resisted the temptation to misuse power themselves, but they did not. It was not long until the powerless became the powerful, and the persecuted became the persecutor.

The whole history of the church reveals that the seduction of power has all too often drawn her off course from her spiritual mission. Wars have been fought, crusades undertaken, inquisitions established, and people burned at the stake because someone capitulated to the illusion that spiritual goals could be accomplished by political means. When the church has seized power in the name of Christ, the very principles of Christ have often been destroyed.

It is in this same manner that our Lord reminded Pilate, "My kingdom is not of this world" (John 18:36). When Pilate became frustrated in questioning Jesus, he threatened, "Don't you realize I have power either to free you or to crucify you?" To which our Lord replied, "You would have no power over me if it were not given to you from above" (John 19:10,11).

The word *power* in this passage translates the Greek word *exousia* (power in the sense of authority). The more familiar word *dunamis* (power in the sense of force or might) is not used in this passage. Therefore, Christ is not threatening Pilate with a display of force; rather, He is reminding him that all human authority is delegated authority, whereas the *exousia* of God is absolute and unrestricted. Thus, true power in the world derives from divine authority and not from political force.

What Power?

It is the threat of political power being used against them that causes most Evangelicals to want to influence or control that power. We tend to be monarchists at heart, who think that if "our" person is in control, then all will go well for us. Many of us forget that our very entrance into politics may degenerate into the use of force (*dunamis*) in the form of political coercion rather than in the pursuit of spiritual power (*exousia*). Without spiritual authority, we cannot hope for much change.

We who claim to trust in the sovereignty of God may at some point have to put that trust to the ultimate test of faith. Just because a professing Christian is running for office does not guarantee the success of his endeavor. Nor does it necessarily mean that he or she is the best candidate for the job. An individual may be a sincere believer but an incompetent politician.

The Scriptures also remind us that there are times that God places the worst of people into political power to accomplish His own goals and purposes. In Daniel 4:17 we read, "The Most High is sovereign over the kingdoms of men and gives them to anyone he wishes and sets over them the lowliest [basest, KJV] of men." This in no way eliminates our personal responsibility for influencing government any more than it did for Daniel.

In fact, Scripture is filled with a wide variety of responses to politics and governance. The judges, for the most part, were miserable failures at human government. Saul lacked the character and skills of leadership. David and Solomon were relatively successful rulers, but each sowed the seeds of future destruction within his own administration. Most of the prophets had strong political opinions about their rulers' personal lives and their administration of justice. Nathan, Elijah, Elisha, Isaiah, and Jeremiah were directly involved in giving advice to political rulers. Daniel, Ezra, Nehemiah, and Esther also served in places of responsibility within hostile pagan governments.

By the time of Christ, people were divided over the issue of politics. The pious wanted to avoid all contamination of contact with Rome. The Herodians promoted total involvement, while the Pharisees and Sadducees preferred limited relations to further their own ends. On the other extreme, the Zealots wanted to overthrow the government by force and usher in the Messiah with an earthly kingdom.

The Divine Enigma

Jesus stood above them all. Like a divine enigma on the landscape of humanity, He seemed to treat the political as mundane. When asked if He would pay the Roman tax, He asked to see the tribute coin. When it was produced, He asked, "Whose is this image and superscription?" (Matthew 22:20 KJV). When He was told it was Caesar's, He merely responded, "Render therefore unto Caesar the things which are Caesar's; and unto God the things that are God's" (Matthew 22:21 KJV).

Jesus always made it clear that the spiritual supersedes the political and that the political derives its authority from the spiritual. It is no wonder that He who was the embodiment of divine authority confounded His captors, accusers, and even the political governor who sentenced Him to die. "I am innocent of the blood of this just person," Pilate protested, as he attempted to wash his hands of the whole matter (see Matthew 27:24 KJV). But no one has ever believed that excuse, and indeed we should not, for the Bible clearly teaches that we are our brother's keeper and responsible under God for the governance of human affairs.

This is the vital truth to which Evangelical Christians must adhere above all else. Might does not necessarily mean we are right. We have often viewed ourselves as a religious minority holding forth against the dragon of unrestricted secularism. But we dare not blow the opportunity by becoming entangled in the mundane affairs of power politics, forgetting that true power (authority) is from God. He is the ultimate source of authority, and He communicates that authority to us when we determine to please Him.

It is our spiritual success, based upon an adherence to God's Word, that restrains the coming of the Antichrist and the False Prophet. Satan's influence in society may seem to be great, but it is, nevertheless, under the restraint of the voice of God through His church. When the church is removed at the rapture, Satan's evil will break completely loose!

Empowered to Witness

In the meantime, there is much to be said in favor of political involvement by the Christian community. Politics, simply defined, is the life of the city (*polis*) and the responsibilities of the citizen (*polites*). British Evangelical John Stott states that in its broadest sense, politics is concerned with "the whole of our life in human society." Therefore, it is "the art of living together in community." In a more narrow sense, he also observes it is the "science of government" whereby the adoption of specific policies are "enshrined in legislation."[21] In this regard, he argues, true Christianity cannot, indeed it dare not, become isolated from society.

Richard Neuhaus has stated that "religion is the heart of culture, culture is the form of religion, and politics is a function of culture."[22] In this sense, religion and politics are inseparable expressions of human culture. He further argues that the culture-forming enterprise in America can be traced back to the nation's Puritan beginnings. However, Evangelical Christians have been largely absent from the process of defining America or setting the moral agenda. But with the abdication of mainline religion from the task of legitimizing the American experiment, Neuhaus believes that the opportunity has passed to the Evangelicals.

When Jesus gave the great commission to evangelize the world to His disciples, He said "All authority [Greek, *exousia*] in heaven and on earth has been given to me" (Matthew 28:18). It is on the basis of that divine authority that He commissions us to be His representatives here on earth. As such, we can neither abdicate the socio-political consequences of discipleship, as did the medieval monastics, nor can we hope to bring about His kingdom on earth by the mere use of political or legal force. Therein lies the tension between religion and politics, and therein must come the solution.

Notice that Jesus said, "All authority . . . has been given to me. Therefore go and make disciples of all nations . . . and surely I am with you always, to the very end of the age" (Matthew 28:18-20). The power of authority was given *to Him*, not us. We are to take His gospel to the world based on His merits, not our own. In Acts 1:8, Jesus told His disciples, "But you will receive power [Greek, *dunamis*, "force"] when the Holy Spirit comes on you; and you will be my witnesses . . . to the ends of the earth."

Notice the proper place of power in the gospel. First, Jesus Christ alone has the authority to send us into the world, and He promises to be with us until the end of this age. Second, He empowers our witness by the baptism of the Holy Spirit so we will recognize that whatever power we seem to have in doing His work is not of ourselves, but of Him. This is the *only* transmission of power that can change the course of history, and it is not limited to political institutions, though it can transform every area of society.

What Can We Do?

We stand at this great moment of history. Concerned about the unprecedented advance of secularism in our society, we cry out against it—but can we really stop it? Evangelical social involvement has brought many issues to the forefront of the public policy debate. Some progress has been made by groups like Focus on the Family, the Christian Coalition, and the Liberty Alliance. But there has been little legislative change that could not be undone by a different administration.

All of this should not surprise us. Believers are citizens of two kingdoms—one heavenly and one earthly. That is why Jesus taught us to pray, "Your will be done on earth as it is in heaven" (Matthew 6:10). As long as we are living on earth, we have a God-given mandate to do all we can to influence this world for the cause of God and Christ. We cannot give up on society merely with the excuse that these are the "last days" so it doesn't matter. We don't know for sure how much time we have left; therefore, we dare not presume on God's timetable.

Jesus told us to evangelize the world until the end of the age (Matthew 28:20). That commission still applies to us until He calls us home in the rapture. In the meantime, secular society is rapidly moving farther away from God and may well be beyond the point of no return.

Let me illustrate this tension between our present responsibility and our ultimate inevitability. Ultimately, this world will vanish away, so why should we be concerned about it? That is like saying, "Why paint your house? It will only need painting again." "Why mow your lawn? It will all burn up one day." "Why exercise? You are going to die anyway." Let's take this a step further. "Why vote? Eventually, the Antichrist will rule the world anyway." "Why evangelize? People really don't want to hear it. Besides, eventually they will all be deceived."

The tension between the here-and-now and the hereafter is as old as the church itself. The apostle Paul had to remind the believers of his day not to become alarmed over this very same thing (2 Thessalonians 2:1). As God's people, we perceive the growing deception of the evil one in our society. Therefore, we must speak out against it. At the same time, however, we realize that the deceiver will eventually win out during the tribulation period. In the meantime, we cannot fatalistically resign ourselves to failure. We have been commissioned by Christ Himself to make a difference in this world until He calls us home.

The old debate between divine sovereignty and human responsibility is at the core of this entire discussion. Some people think if God is going to do whatever He is going to do anyway, why bother? But God has chosen to work through His people to accomplish His will. God does the saving, but He tells us to be His witnesses.

We do not know the timetable of God, but we can all smell the ashes of a decadent society that may soon face extinction. It is only a matter of time until the human race faces the prospect of annihilation. But first, the deceiver will arise, promising to bring peace to the world.

Spiritual darkness threatens to engulf us. False prophets are everywhere. The world is rushing headlong toward disaster. We dare not give up until the trumpet sounds, and we all go home to glory. We must keep our spiritual balance between our present earthly life and our future hope as we approach the end of the age.

10

Prophecies of
the End Times

*When these things begin to take
place . . . lift up your heads, because
your redemption is drawing near.*

—Luke 21:28

The Bible is filled with prophetic statements about
future events. The Old Testament predicts the rise and fall
of nations and rulers by name. The biblical prophecies tell
of future events that will impact Israel, Egypt, Babylon, and
Rome. The New Testament predicts the fall of Jerusalem,
the coming tribulation, the rise of the Antichrist, and the
battle of Armageddon.

In the Old Testament, the central feature of prophecy is
the coming of Messiah (Christ). In the New Testament, the
central feature of prophecy is the second coming of Christ.
In the Old Testament, we are told that He will be born of a

virgin (Isaiah 7:14) in the city of Bethlehem (Micah 5:2), He will rule on the throne of David (Isaiah 9:7), and He will die for our sins (Isaiah 53:7,8) and be pierced through (Zechariah 12:10). In the New Testament, Jesus predicted He would rise again on the third day (Matthew 16:21). He also predicted He would come again (John 14:3). Jesus said, "I have told you now before it happens, so that when it does happen you will believe" (John 14:29).

The prophecies of Christ's first coming were literally fulfilled with such exact accuracy that we can assume the prophecies of His second coming will be fulfilled in like manner. The major prophecies pointing to our Lord's return emphasize the literal nature of His second coming, the time of apostasy before His return, the rapture of the church, and the coming world empire of the Antichrist.

Wars and Rumors of Wars

On the headquarters of the United Nations in New York, there is inscribed the words of Micah 4:3 (KJV):

> . . . and they shall beat their swords into plow-shares, and their spears into pruninghooks: nation shall not lift up a sword against nation, neither shall they learn war any more.

This will only be realized when the Prince of Peace comes to reign on this earth. Both Daniel and Jesus warned of continual war until the return of Christ (Daniel 9:26; Matthew 24:6). It has been pointed out by the Society of International Law at London that there have been only 268 years of peace during the last 4,000 years of human history—despite the signing of more than 8,000 separate peace treaties!

In February 1914, a prophecy conference sponsored by Bible-believing people was held in Los Angeles. When the sessions were completed, a religious magazine entitled *The Christian Advocate* sneeringly dubbed this prophecy gathering a "pathetic conference" because it held that wars would continue to intensify until the advent of Christ.

But the sneers soon disappeared, for in August of that very year, the guns of World War I commenced their deadly thunder. World War II, Korea, Vietnam, and the Gulf War have followed. The missiles of destruction continue to this day!

Until the coming of Christ, the UN would have been more correct by inscribing the fearful words of Joel 3:9,10 (KJV):

> Proclaim ye this among the Gentiles; prepare war, wake up the mighty men, let all the men of war draw near; let them come up: Beat your plowshares into swords, and your pruninghooks into spears.

It has been calculated by a former president of the Norwegian Academy of Sciences, aided by historians from England, Egypt, Germany, and India, that since 3600 B.C. over 14,531 wars have been waged in which 3,640,000,000 people have been killed. That figure is more than 17 times the entire population of the United States! The value of this destruction would pay for a golden highway around the world some 90 miles in width and 33 feet thick.

By far the most costly in terms of human life was World War II (1939–1945), in which the total number of fatalities, including battle deaths and civilians of all countries, is estimated to have been 54,800,000. The country that suffered most was Poland, with 6,028,000 or 22.2 percent of its population killed. The material cost of World War II has been estimated at $3.5 trillion. If this cost could be pro-rated among the people of the world, the amount for each man, woman, boy, and girl would be $1,708. This amount is exclusive of loss of lives and property.

Rebirth of Modern Israel

The tiny nation of Israel is the geographical focal point of Bible prophecy. On April 6, 1917, America entered World War I. In July of that year, British General Sir Edmund Allenby was appointed commander of the allied armies in Palestine. On November 16, the fortified coastal city of Jaffa was taken, leaving Jerusalem open for attack. On December 8, British troops arrived at Jerusalem. This was the day of the Jewish feast of Hanukkah, which com-memorated the deliverance of Jerusalem by the Maccabees in the year 165 B.C. Early Sunday morning, December 9, the Turks began fleeing the city without firing a shot. Thus, after being ruled over by the Turks, whose very symbol of authority was that of a slashing sword, the Holy City now came under British protection.

During the 30 years of British control of Palestine, hos-tilities continued between the Arab and Israeli population. But after World War II, the British determined to relinquish control of Palestine, giving part of the land to Israel and part to Jordan. Early in 1948, Britain announced it would evacuate Palestine in May.

At sunrise on May 14, 1948, Great Britain's flag, the Union Jack, was hauled down from its staff over the Gov-ernment House in Jerusalem. The presiding British High Commissioner, Sir Allen Gorden Cunningham, then left the Holy Land for the last time amid a 17-gun salute. The 30-year British rule was over.

Shortly before 4:00 P.M. that same day, David Ben-Gurion drove down Rothschild Boulevard in Tel Aviv and entered a white, modern, two-story building to attend a meeting with some 400 individuals. This number included Jewish religious and political leaders and many representatives of the local and worldwide press. At exactly 4:00 P.M., Ben-Gurion called the meeting to order. The assembly arose and sang the Jewish national anthem, while in an adjoining room, the Palestine symphony orchestra played.

Declaration of Independence

In Jerusalem, over 100,000 Jews listened by radio to the Tel Aviv ceremonies, unable to attend, being cut off and surrounded by Arab armies. The music had hardly ceased when Ben-Gurion rose and, in a firm, strong, emphatic voice read in Hebrew the Declaration of Independence of the new State of Israel. Israel's first prime minister stood under a portrait of Theodor Herzel and read the historic 697-word document in 17 minutes. Some of the key paragraphs in this proclamation of freedom read as follows:[1]

- In the Land of Israel the Jewish people came into being. In this land was shaped their spiritual, religious and national character. Here they lived in sovereign independence. Here they created a culture of national and universal import, and gave to the world the eternal Book of Books. . . .

- Exiled by force, still the Jewish people kept faith with their land in all the countries of their dispersion, steadfast in their prayer and hope to return and here revive their political freedom. . . .

• Accordingly we, the members of the National
Council, representing the Jewish people in the
Land of Israel and the Zionist Movement, have
assembled on the day of the termination of the
British mandate for Palestine, and, by virtue of
our natural and historic right and of the resolu-
tion of the General Assembly of the United
Nations, do hereby proclaim the establishment
of a Jewish State in the Land of Israel—the State
of Israel. . . .

• We trust in the Rock of Israel, we set our hands
in witness to this proclamation, at this session of
the Provisional Council of State, on the soil of
the Homeland, in the city of Tel Aviv, the Sab-
bath eve, the fifth day of Iyar, 5708, the four-
teenth day of May, nineteen hundred and
forty-eight.

At 5:00 P.M. on that same day in New York, a special
emergency meeting of the UN General Assembly was held
to consider the war clouds of the Middle East that would
certainly unleash their fury at 6:00 New York time (midnight in Palestine). They had one hour to do something.
Suddenly, an amazing and totally unexpected news bulletin
from Washington, D.C., was received at the UN. President
Harry Truman had just recognized the new Jewish State.
The time was 6:11 P.M. in New York, but six hours later in
Jerusalem. Truman thus recognized the Israeli State just 11
minutes after it had come into existence! His message read
as follows:

This government has been informed that a Jewish
State has been proclaimed in Palestine, and recog-
nition has been requested by the Provisional Government thereof. The United States Government

recognizes the Provisional Government the "de facto" authority of the New State of Israel.

Three days later, on May 18, Russia recognized Israel. Thus, for the first time since September 8, A.D. 70, the Holy Land officially belonged to the Jews. Israel had been reborn in her ancient land in fulfillment of biblical prophecy.

Struggle to Survive

Israel's *War of Independence* began on November 29, 1947, and continued (with some interruption) until February 24, 1949. On May 15, 1948, Israel was invaded by Egypt, Jordan, Iraq, Syria, and Lebanon. This pitted some 45 million Arabs against 100,000 Jews. They closed in from the north, south, and east, while Israel's back was to the Mediterranean Sea in the west.

Against insurmountable odds, Israel defended herself against the onslaught and eventually emerged victoriously. It was an incredible victory. At no other time in history had so few people defeated so many. After 2,500 years of oppression and dispersion, the nation of Israel was reborn in her original homeland.

By 1952, the population of Israel doubled, and it has been exploding ever since. Today, over 6 million Jews live in Israel. Immigration projects were set up all over the world. Operation Magic Carpet airlifted 50,000 Jews from Yemen, on the Arabian peninsula. Another spectacular airlift brought over 100,000 Jews from Baghdad, Iraq, in Operation Ali Baba. These were descendants of the Jews who were taken into captivity by Nebuchadnezzar of Babylon.

Later wars brought even more success and more immigration to Israel. The *Sinai War* began October 29 and ended on November 5, 1956. Within one week the fast-moving Israeli forces had overrun the entire Sinai Peninsula and destroyed the Egyptian army. The *Six Day War* began on June 5 and ended by June 10, 1967. In one of the most spectacular military engagements in history, Israel destroyed the combined air forces of Egypt, Jordan, and Syria. The Israelis also captured the Gaza Strip, West Bank, Golan Heights, the Sinai, and the old city of Jerusalem. The *Yom Kippur War* began on October 6 and ended on October 25, 1973. Israel was attacked simultaneously by Egypt and Syria on her sacred Day of Atonement. Again, Israel won decisively.

During the *Gulf War* of 1991, Iraq attacked Israel with SCUD missiles, but the Israelis showed restraint by staying out of the way, allowing the U.S.-coalition forces to defeat Iraq.

Each of these conflicts was unsuccessful in eliminating the tiny nation of Israel. It should be obvious by now that she is back in her land by a miracle of God. The prophet Amos promised: "I will bring back my exiled people Israel; they will rebuild the ruined cities and live in them. . . . I will plant Israel in their own land, never again to be uprooted from the land I have given them" (Amos 9:14,15). God is clearly fulfilling His promise. I am convinced that the literal fulfillment of these prophecies is intended to strengthen our confidence in all of God's prophecies about future events. He has spoken about many things that must be taken seriously if we are to understand the future.

Revived Roman Empire

The Bible not only predicts the restoration of Israel (see Ezekiel 37), but also the revival of the old Roman Empire

(Daniel 2:41; 7:7,8; Revelation 13:1; 17:12). During the Olivet Discourse, Jesus said: "Jerusalem will be trampled on by the Gentiles until the times of the Gentiles are fulfilled" (Luke 21:24). This time began when Nebuchadnezzar of Babylon conquered Jerusalem in 586 B.C. and has continued until the present time. Although the Jews have had control of Jerusalem since 1967, they still do not control the Temple Mount (where the Dome of the Rock presently stands).

I believe the Bible clearly predicts the resurgence of Europe as the revived Roman Empire of the future. This is the final phase of Daniel's fourth kingdom in his prophecies of the end times (Daniel 2 and 7). This revived Roman Empire will consist of ten units and will eventually be controlled by the Antichrist, who will attempt to sign a peace treaty with Israel (Daniel 9:27).

It is quite probable that the Antichrist will even encourage the Jews to rebuild the temple and institute animal sacrifices. Whatever his relationship to Israel, he will eventually break his covenant and turn against her. This is symbolized in Revelation 12 by the persecution of the woman (Israel) who is forced to flee into the wilderness.

As noted in chapter 8, the book of Revelation refers symbolically to this final kingdom as "Babylon." But it is not likely referring to ancient Babylon (Iraq). The prophetic "Babylon" of the future sits on seven hills (Revelation 17:9) and "rules over the kings of the earth" (17:18). It is the center of the great material, economic, and political system of the last days. There can be little doubt that John is using the term *Babylon* to symbolize Rome and the European Union. Whether this includes the United States is mere speculation.

Rapture of the Church

The rapture involves Christ's return for the church. The Bible clearly states, "The Lord himself will come down from heaven . . . and the dead in Christ will rise first. After that, we who are still alive and are left will be *caught up* together with them in the clouds to meet the Lord in the air" (1 Thessalonians 4:16,17, emphasis added). In the rapture, both those who have died in Christ over the centuries and those who are alive when He returns will be taken up. This is the church's hope. She awaits the Savior who is coming for His bride.

The church may endure persecution, trouble, and difficulty, but she is not the object of divine wrath. The church does not await destruction as the world does. Rather, she awaits the coming of her Lord and King. Peter explains that the present world is "reserved for fire, being kept for the day of judgment and destruction of *ungodly* men" (2 Peter 3:7 KJV, emphasis added). The church is pictured in Scripture as the wife of the Lamb (Revelation 19:7-9). He may discipline her in love, but His ultimate purpose is to present her to the Father as His perfect bride.

The concept of the rapture is expressed in the biblical terms *caught up* (Greek, *harpazo*) and *gathered together* (Greek, *episunagoges)*. Hogg and Vine observe that *harpazo* is the same verb used of Paul ("whether it was in the body or out of the body . . . caught up," 2 Corinthians 12:2-4); Philip ("Spirit . . . caught away Philip," Acts 8:39 KJV); and the man child ("caught up unto God," Revelation 12:5 KJV).[2] This explains that *harpazo* conveys the idea of force suddenly exercised and is best rendered "snatch" (John 10:28,29 NIV), where Jesus promises that "no one can snatch them out of my hand." He alone does the snatching at the time of the rapture!

By contrast, *episunagoges* refers to that which results from the "catching up" *(harpazo)*. Once caught up into the clouds, we shall be gathered together with the Lord. In commenting on 2 Thessalonians 2:1, Hogg and Vine observe: "Here it refers to the 'rapture' of the saints into the air to meet and to be forever with the Lord."[3] The basic meaning is to "assemble together." The raptured church is pictured as the great "assembly" (synagogue) in the sky. George Milligan observes: "The word goes back to the saying of the Lord in Mark 13:27 ("gather together His elect"), and is found elsewhere in the New Testament only in Hebrews 10:25, where it is applied to the ordinary religious assembling of believers as an anticipation of the great assembling at the Lord's coming.[4]

There can be no valid system of biblical eschatology without a rapture. The church will be "caught up" and "gathered together" with her Lord. The only real debate is when. Any eschatological system that dismisses the rapture as some hoax has forfeited the essential biblical teaching that Christ will come and snatch away His bride to the great assembly in heaven.

Jesus will come in the clouds to rapture the church. He will come for those who are living at the time of His return; He will come for every believer. The Scripture promises: "We will *all* be changed" (1 Corinthians 15:51, emphasis added). The church will be raptured to the marriage supper of the Lamb (Revelation 19:7).

The Tribulation Period

In the meantime, all the fury of Satan will be unleashed on the earth. The Bible calls this period of time "the day of the Lord" (1 Thessalonians 5:2 KJV) or the "time of Jacob's trouble" (Jeremiah 30:7 KJV) or "the great day of his wrath" (Revelation 6:17 KJV).

Dr. Willmington notes:

> According to the Bible there is coming a calamity unlike any which this weary world has ever seen. Although this future period will be relatively short, it will nevertheless destroy more of this earth's population than all previous disasters combined.[5]

The Lord Jesus described it like this: "For then there will be great distress, unequaled from the beginning of the world until now—and never to be equaled again. If those days had not been cut short, no one would survive" (Matthew 24:21,22). The Bible describes this as a time of worldwide conflict and devastation, resulting in air and water pollution, deforestation of the planet, and the near destruction of mankind (see Revelation 6–8).

Jesus predicted signs in heavens, disaster and distress on earth, and spiritual conflict behind the scenes. So terrible will be these judgments that people will pray to die. They will pray to the rocks to "fall on us and hide us from the face of him who sits on the throne and from the wrath of the Lamb! For the great day of their wrath has come, and who can stand?" (Revelation 6:16,17).

In describing the events of the tribulation period, Ed Dobson observes: "Jesus identified two kinds of signs that will point to the end of the world and His coming: natural signs and spiritual signs.[6]

A. *Natural Signs*

1. wars

2. famines

3. earthquakes

B. *Spiritual Signs*

1. false christs

2. persecution of believers

3. martyrdom

4. people turning from the faith

5. false prophets

6. people's love will grow cold

7. gospel will be preached in the whole world

The tribulation period will be marked by three significant events that will change the course of human history.

1. ***Abomination of Desolation*** (Matthew 24:15): This incident will mirror the desecration of the temple by Antiochus IV Epiphanes in 168 B.C., when he sacrificed a pig on the altar of the temple. This false "abomination" will occur when the Antichrist presents himself to be worshiped as God in the temple (see 2 Thessalonians 2:4). Desmond Ford notes the parallel to Revelation 17, where the Antichrist is depicted as the "mother of harlots and abominations of the earth." He who has desolated others will ultimately be made "desolate" himself.[7]

2. ***Cataclysmic Signs*** (Matthew 24:29): Biblical prophecy predicts such cataclysmic events as the darkening of the sun, moon, and stars. Dobson notes that this "may describe the aftermath of nuclear destruction, when the air is filled with dust particles that hide the light of the sun. Or this could be the direct action of God shaking the foundations of the

universe. In either case, the events are massive in their impact."[8]

3. *Coming of Jesus Christ:* The great tribulation will conclude with the return of Jesus Christ. He will come with the army of heaven (the church and the angelic host) to confront the Antichrist at the battle of Armageddon. His decisive victory will defeat the "evil trinity": Satan, Antichrist, and the False Prophet (Revelation 19:19–20:2). Christ's triumph will mark the final turning point of human history. After that, the triumphal outcome (despite Satan's final rebellion—Revelation 20:7-10) will be assured.

The Battle of Armageddon

The Antichrist will rise to power, promising to bring peace to Israel and to the whole world. His rise will probably be spurred on by continuing conflicts in the Middle East and the need to ensure worldwide peace. But his attempts at peace will fail, and he will turn to military action for enforcement. Tragically, this will only stimulate further conflict.

A series of wars will culminate at Armageddon (Revelation 16:16). The battlefield will stretch from Megiddo, on the north to Edom, on the south, a distance of over 200 miles. It will encompass the valleys of Megiddo, Esdraelon, and Jehoshaphat (see Joel 3:2,12; Zechariah 12:11). Here, in the very area where so many biblical battles were fought, the last great conflict will ensue. The armies of the world's last great powers will assemble only to be destroyed at the return of Christ. At the point of annihilation Jesus will return to save the world.

Having already raptured the church to heaven seven years earlier, we are told that Christ will return with His church triumphant (Revelation 19:11-16). And *"after* the tribulation of those days shall the sun be darkened . . . and the powers of the heavens shall be shaken" (Matthew 24:29, emphasis added). The prophet Zechariah predicts that Christ will return to the Mount of Olives and split it apart (Zechariah 14:4).

Zechariah also predicts the future conversion of Israel to faith in Christ during that time:

> I will pour upon the house of David, and upon the inhabitants of Jerusalem, the spirit of grace and supplications: and they shall look upon me whom they have pierced, and they shall mourn for him, as one mourneth for his only son. . . . in that day shall there be a great mourning in Jerusalem . . . in the valley of Megiddon (Zechariah 12:10,11 KJV).

Great and terrible judgments are coming upon those who have rejected Christ and His saving grace. Today God is still patiently waiting for mankind to repent and turn to Him, but there is coming a day when He will withdraw His grace and respond in judgment. When that comes, it will be worse than anything the world has ever known.

The Millennial Kingdom

After Armageddon, Christ will cast the beast (Antichrist) and the False Prophet into the lake of fire (Revelation 19:20). Then He will bind Satan for 1,000 years in the bottomless pit (Revelation 20:1-3). During the thousand years, Christ will rule on the earth with His resurrected and raptured saints in the millennial kingdom (Revelation 20:4).

In Revelation 20, John mentions the 1,000-year period no less than six times. It is equated with the reign of Christ on earth and the binding of Satan. Rene Pache notes that the Jewish Talmud also speaks of a 1,000-year messianic kingdom.[9]

During His kingdom on earth, our Lord will reward the righteous, vindicate the truth, and set the record of history straight. The promise of "glory to follow" will be fulfilled. Worldwide peace will finally become a reality when the Prince of peace reigns on the earth. During this time, the reign of Christ will radiate the glory of God to all nations. It will be a time harmony, joy, and holiness.

The curse of sin on the natural world will be removed, sicknesses will be healed, hatreds will be forgiven, and animosities will be removed. The lion shall lie down with the lamb. Christ Himself will reign supreme in peace and prosperity for all who acknowledge Him: "Every knee should bow . . . and every tongue confess that Jesus Christ is Lord" (Philippians 2:10,11).

You and I cannot imagine what that will be like. To live in a world where there is no war, virtually no crime, no rebellion is almost heaven on earth. Yet, at the end of the millennial kingdom, Satan will be loosed again for a brief time and will gather a rebellious host to follow him against the personal reign of Christ on earth. Despite God's blessings for a thousand years, some will choose to reject Christ and follow Satan (see Revelation 20:7-10). This last desperate act of unregenerate hearts will confirm the absolute depravity of mankind once and for all.

The insurrection will be overthrown by God Himself: "Fire came down from heaven and devoured them" (Revelation 20:9). Satan is then cast into the lake of fire, where the beast and False Prophet have been for 1,000 years. The insurrection is followed by the great white throne judgment when Christ Himself judges the unbelieving world (Revelation 20:11-15). Everyone not found in the book of life will be cast into the lake of fire. This is the final judgment.

New Heavens and Earth

The promise of a new heaven and a new earth are first recorded in the Old Testament by the prophet Isaiah. He said, "Behold, I will create new heavens and a new earth. The former things will not be remembered, nor will they come to mind" (Isaiah 65:17). Isaiah went on to predict a New Jerusalem (65:18), as well as a time when there would be no tears, pain, or death. In so doing, Isaiah saw further into the future than any other Old Testament prophet.

Isaiah also says, " 'As the new heavens and the earth that I make will endure before me,' declares the LORD, 'so will your name and descendants endure' " (66:22). This is the eternal kingdom of God where we shall live forever. The redeemed are in a final state of blessing and righteousness. By contrast, Isaiah 66:24 also makes it clear that the unrighteous are in a state of final punishment.

Isaiah's vision of the future also included a time when the millions of redeemed people from all of human history would come and worship before the Lord perpetually. Eternity is pictured as a place of activity and service. It is a place of blessing where we are continually praising and serving God. There will be no temple in the eternal city because God and Christ (the Lamb) are the temple. There will be no sun or moon in the eternal city because the glory of God and the Lamb will light it. In fact there is no night there (Revelation 21:22-27). But there is the river of life and the tree of life (Revelation 22:1,2). It is paradise restored as it was intended originally for Adam and Eve.

This is something beyond the millennial kingdom and its temporary splendor. This is the eternal kingdom of God, where we shall "reign forever and ever" (Revelation 22:5). The present earth and heavens (atmosphere) will be destroyed and replaced by a new earth and new heavens. Jesus said, "Heaven and earth will pass away, but my words will never pass away" (Matthew 24:35).

The apostle Peter put it this way: "But the day of the Lord will come as a thief in the night; in which the heavens shall pass away with a great noise, and the elements shall melt with fervent heat, the earth also and the works that are therein shall be burned up" (2 Peter 3:10 KJV). In God's final fiery refinement, the creation will be purged from the stains of sin.

In light of our eternal destiny, Peter wrote: "But in keeping with his promise we are looking forward to a new heaven and a new earth, the home of righteousness" (2 Peter 3:13). It is this hope of a better world to come that enables believers to handle the heartaches and disappointments of life here and now.

Living in Light of Eternity

Peter also reminds us that in the last days, scoffers will come questioning the second coming of Christ, saying "Where is the promise of his coming?" (2 Peter 3:4 KJV). It has now been nearly 2,000 years since our Lord ascended back to heaven. The church has been waiting all this time for her final redemption. We dare not lose hope now, when we are so much closer to the end than we have ever been. Since we do have the hope of our Lord's return and of a better world to come, Peter says, "So then, dear friends, since you are looking forward to this, make every effort to be found spotless, blameless and at peace with him" (2 Peter 3:14).

The apostle John expressed the same concern in writing about the second coming of Christ when "we shall be like him, for we shall see him as he is" (1 John 3:2). John looks forward to this glorious appearing of Christ and then adds the admonition, "Everyone who has this hope in him purifies himself, just as he is pure" (3:3).

If we really believe that Jesus Christ is coming again to rapture the church, judge the world, set up his kingdom, and rule for all eternity, then we ought to live like it! Many Christians lose sight of their eternal destiny. They become bogged down with the mundane problems of life and allow themselves to become worried, depressed, angry, or confused. Why? Because they forget whose they are and what their final destiny is really all about.

If we really kept our perspective on eternity, we would not let the problems of earth get us down. But the temptation to focus on the temporal, instead of the eternal, is a constant struggle for all of us. Whether our daily problems revolve around our health, finances, family, friends, career, or temporal security, true Christians must look beyond all of these things to the only real source of security in our lives—Jesus Christ!

Our Lord spent most of His earthly life trying to help His disciples get their eyes off the temporal and on the eternal. He also spent a great deal of time focusing on the spiritual as opposed to the material. In the process, He teaches us about true contentment.

The truth is that we have more life ahead of us than we do behind us. No matter how old we are right now, we have a great future ahead! It includes the *greatest events in biblical prophecy:*

- rapture of the church
- marriage supper of the Lamb
- triumphal return with Christ
- millennial kingdom on earth
- eternal reign in heaven
- new heaven and new earth

We have more life ahead of us than behind us. Christ has planned a glorious future for His children. Every born-again believer will participate in these incredible events that are yet to come. Keep looking up; the Savior is coming!

How Close Is the End?

Then they gathered the kings together
to the place that in Hebrew is called
Armageddon.

—Revelation 16:16

Evangelical Christians believe that we are living in the end times, when the world will enter into a series of cataclysmic wars. By the time the wars end, perhaps as much as three-fourths of the earth's population will be destroyed. These chilling events will precede the triumphant return of Christ to earth.

"Armageddon theology" is the popular term for an eschatological understanding of biblical prophecy about the end of the world. In secular America, these beliefs are little understood, but in Christian circles they are heatedly discussed on a regular basis. Some 50 million Americans who call themselves "born again" Christians agree with the basic tenets of that eschatology. Hal Lindsey's book *The Late Great Planet Earth*, which expresses the Evangelical understanding of the future, has sold over 30 million copies.[1] Messages on Bible prophecy have been proclaimed over the television airwaves by preachers such as Jerry Falwell, Pat Robertson, John Hagee, and Jack Van Impe. And if Evangelical involvement in the political process continues to grow, it is likely that Armageddon theology will also gain increasing exposure.

During the 1984 presidential debates, Ronald Reagan was asked by Marvin Kalb, "Do you feel that we are now heading, perhaps, for some kind of nuclear Armageddon?" The former president responded that he had spoken with theologians who felt that biblical prophecies were being fulfilled as never before. But "no one knows whether those prophecies mean that Armageddon is a thousand years away or the day after tomorrow. So I have never seriously warned and said we must plan according to Armageddon."[2] If Reagan's degree of agreement with the theologians is uncertain, his affirmation of the inevitability of such a conflict was to many a shocking admission.

For a variety of reasons, the notion of Armageddon theology is deeply troubling to many Christians, Jews, and secularists. Their concern surfaced recently when 100 religious leaders, including William Sloane Coffin and Bishop Thomas Gumbleton, held a press conference to announce that it was profoundly disturbing that political leaders "might identify with extremists who believe that nuclear war is inevitable and imminent." After all, this could easily lead one to conclude that reconciliation with America's adversaries is ultimately futile. The liberal Christic Institute went further, charging that Evangelicals were using prophecy "to justify nuclear war as a divine instrument to punish the wicked and complete God's plan for history."[3]

Apparently many believe that because Evangelicals look forward to the second coming of Christ, they will try to hasten that event. They are often accused of trying to foment a crisis in the Middle East that could lead to a war with Israel or provoke a showdown between the major super powers. Some people who understand the belief that born again Christians will be raptured or taken out of the world before the final tribulation charge that believers are indifferent to peace-making efforts, since they do not think they will suffer the consequences of the war of Armageddon.[4]

Christians who believe the forces of God will triumph ultimately over the forces of evil sometimes ask why Evangelicals would hesitate to get into a war they are theologically assured of winning. Finally, there is a general concern about the widespread conversion of non-Christians, especially Jews, which is said to attend the end times. These arguments, however, are based on a profound misunderstanding of the Bible and what Evangelicals actually believe. In order to understand this issue, it is important to understand something of the history of biblical prophecy.

Views of Eschatology

Both the Old and New Testaments speak about the end of the world. The prophet Joel called it the "day of the LORD." He foresaw a day of thick darkness, gloominess, clouds, and a devouring fire (see Joel 2:1-3). The prophet Isaiah called it the "day of the Lord's vengence" (see Isaiah 34:9 KJV). As I've noted before, the apostle Peter predicted "the elements shall melt with fervent heat, the earth also and the works that are therein shall be burned up" (2 Peter 3:10 KJV). The apostle Paul warned that "the Lord Jesus shall be revealed from heaven with his mighty angels, in flaming fire taking vengeance on them that know not God" (2 Thessalonians 1:7,8 KJV). The book of Revelation says the air will be darkened, water polluted, and great rivers dried up. Earthquakes will shake the planet, and Babylon will be devoured by fire. Concurrent with these visions of destruction are prophecies of the coming millennial, the 1,000-year reign of Jesus Christ.

For centuries, Christians have tried to attach dates to these prophecies, with a spectacular lack of success. As early as the second century A.D., Montanus predicted that Christ would soon return to set up His kingdom in Phrygia in Asia Minor. Since then, other candidates for the New Jerusalem have included Rome, Constantinople, London, Münster (Germany), and Chicago. The Mormons think it will be Salt Lake City, although one vocal group of Mormon dissidents insists it will be Independence, Missouri.[5]

One Puritan writer said that Christ would return in 1666.[6] When that didn't happen, another extended the deadline to 1690.[7] In the aftermath of the Reformation, a group of Christians took over Münster. Their parliament actually held debates on whether a man on horseback seen riding through the area was Christ returned to earth.[8] When French troops temporarily drove the pope from Rome in 1798, one millennialist predicted that the battle of Armageddon had already begun with the forces of Antichrist.[9]

In the early nineteenth century, a Baptist preacher named William Miller predicted that Christ would return in 1844; Miller arrived at that date by converting the 2,300 days of Daniel 8:14 into years. When 1844 passed, Miller gave up on the scheme, but many of his followers did not—they formed what later became known as the Seventh-day Adventists.[10] At the end of the nineteenth century, Charles Russell predicted that Christ would return visibly in 1914. He didn't, so his followers—who called themselves the Jehovah's Witnesses—claimed Christ came secretly and ushered in the Kingdom Age. Thus, Jehovah's Witnesses meet in "kingdom halls."[11]

Our own century has seen its share of date-setting and millennial predictions. Herbert Armstrong declared that the end of the world would come in January 1972, and some of his followers promptly sold their possessions and took to the hills.[12] Others predicted that Soviet communists would invade the United States in 1976. The symbol 666 from the book of Revelation has been identified with Hitler, Mussolini, Franklin Roosevelt, Henry Kissinger, and a host of others—including Ronald Wilson Reagan, whose three names all have six letters. In the face of all this, it may seem hard to take biblical prophecy seriously at all. But Evangelicals do.

In understanding the Evangelical view of biblical prophecy, it is crucial to define *three different systems of eschatology.* Each views the end times very differently, and consequently their political implications are quite different.

The **postmillennial** school believes that Christ will return after the millennium to announce that His kingdom on earth has been realized. Postmillennialists believe that during the millennium, the church should conquer unbelief and convert the vast majority of people to Christianity. They also believe that society should be run according to biblical law. In this way, they seek to usher in the second coming of Christ. Postmillennial advocates have included Catholics, Puritans, and some modern-day fundamentalists and charismatics. They emphasize "Dominion Theology" and argue that Christians are to take dominion over the earth in order to actualize the kingdom of God on earth.[13]

Amillennial theology sees no literal millennium on earth. It tends to view events described in the book of Revelation as referring to the Church Age—the time when Christianity exerts a powerful influence on people and overcomes the forces of evil. References to the "thousand years" are interpreted as symbolic. Amillennialists believe that Christ will return and immediately conduct the last judgment. Two elements of amillennialism are preeminent in its eschatology. First, all of God's promises to Israel are viewed as being fulfilled in the New Testament church. Thus, amillennialists see no specific future for national Israel. Instead, they view the church as "spiritual" Israel. Second, amillennialists have traditionally argued for an extensive involvement of the church in cultural, social, and political affairs. They view the present era as the ultimate conflict between the forces of good and evil.[14]

Finally there is *premillennialism,* which holds that Christ will return before the millennium and then reign on the earth for 1,000 years. Most premillennialists do not believe Christians will be present on earth during the last days to witness the war, tribulation, and the Christian conversion of the Jews. Because premillennialists do not believe that society must be prepared for 1,000 years for Christ's second coming, they reject the idea of imposing biblical law on unbelievers. Premillennialists are by far the dominant strain in Evangelical eschatology.[15] Traditionally premillennialists have avoided any involvement in American political and social issues. Those who also believe in a pretribulational rapture generally have been content to wait for Christ to come and remove the church from this evil society.

We should further note that *premillennialists* are themselves subdivided into three camps:

1. **Pretribulationalists** believe that Christ will return in the air to rapture the church before the tribulation begins on earth. After seven years of tribulation, Christ will return with His church to defeat the forces of Antichrist and establish the kingdom of God on earth.[16]

2. **Midtribulationalists** believe that the church will go through the first three-and-one-half years of the tribulation period and be raptured at the midpoint of the seven years of total tribulation. Those advocating this view emphasize the prophetic use of the phrase "time, times, and a half a time" to refer to three-and-one-half years.[17]

3. **Posttribulationalists** believe the church will go through the entire seven-year tribulation period on earth at the end of the present Church Age. Thus, these interpreters view the suffering "saints" in the prophecies of Revelation as Christians, not converted Jews.[18]

With such diverse Evangelical opinion, it is folly to label any one view as *the* Evangelical eschatology. Unfortunately, this is often done by the media because of the popularization of the pretribulational and premillennial views of the most popular television preachers. Of all the TV pastors, only James Kennedy and Robert Schuller shy away from this position, preferring the amillennial perspective.[19] They believe that God's promises to Israel were allegorically fulfilled in the New Israel, that is, the Christian church. Pretribulationists on television include Jerry Falwell, John Hagee, Charles Stanley, Jack Van Impe, Peter and Paul Lalonde, Richard Lee, and Hal Lindsey.

Postmillennial Visions of a New Theocracy

Apocalyptic visions of the end of the world are nothing new. They have played an important role throughout church history and have been especially predominant in the history of the Protestant movement. As early as the Middle Ages, John Wycliffe (1329–1384) suggested that the Catholic pope was the Antichrist and that Protestants were engaged in an apocalyptic war with the corrupted papacy.[20] This idea greatly influenced John Calvin and Martin Luther. Many Protestant reformers identified the years A.D. 500 to A.D. 1500 as the millennium of the "legitimate papacy," after which they felt it was corrupted by Satan. These reformers believed the Reformation represented an attempt by Protestants to expel the satanic evil before the final conflict of Armageddon.[21]

The early reformers also viewed these years as the 1,000 years when Satan was bound on earth (see Revelation 20:1-3). During this time the spread of the gospel flourished in Europe. Using this scheme, they further surmised that Satan was now loosed to deceive the nations.

The reformers believed they were engaged in the final, apocalyptic struggle with Satan and the forces of Antichrist. For example, the Puritans were postmillennialists who believed they were living in the last part of the 1,000 years after which Christ would come. The Cromwellian revolution was, to them, the "Battle of Gog and Magog"— in other words, the final conflict. Puritans called for the complete expulsion of the forces of Antichrist embodied in the monarch Charles I. The notable Puritan divine, John Owen, told Parliament that Charles' execution was a "fulfillment of prophecy."[22]

But Charles died and Christ did not return. Soon Puritan eschatology began to shift from postmillennialism toward premillennialism. No longer was the church seen as a mechanism for bringing about Christ's second coming. Hope was placed, instead, in waiting for Christ, who would fulfill what the church had failed to accomplish.[23]

The New World saw a revival of postmillennialism. Puritans in America identified their country with the New Jerusalem, and they believed God would establish His kingdom on earth on America's shores. During the Great Awakening of the 1740s, Jonathan Edwards enthusiastically predicted that the millennium was coming to an end and that Christ would return shortly; this millennial enthusiasm played an important role in the American Revolution.[24]

Postmillennialism remained a dominant force in American Protestantism throughout the eighteenth and nineteenth centuries. But postmillennialist notions of a world bringing itself more into line with God to prepare for His return were shattered by twentieth-century catastrophes such as the Nazi holocaust and Stalin's genocide. Far from moving toward greater conversion and a closer following of biblical law, the world seemed to be moving away from it. By the mid-twentieth century, postmillennialism was fading.

One exception to this trend was Rousas J. Rushdoony and his Chalcedon group. Rushdoony is a highly regarded biblical scholar who advocates the reconstruction of American society based upon biblical law. An early supporter of the Moral Majority, Rushdoony not only advocates the necessity of Christian influence in society, but the total conquest of society by Christians.[25]

Rushdoony wants to replace secular law with biblical law. He has outlined his vision in *Institute of Biblical Law*, regarded as his masterwork. In it he calls for "the saints of the world," that is, Christians, "to prepare to take over the world's government and its courts." Rushdoony distrusts democracy; in fact, he maintains that "the choice, ultimately, is the basic one between democracy and traditional Christian theology." He believes Christians must use the democratic process to come to power, and then end democracy. Some of Rushdoony's followers, in order to prepare the world for Christ's second coming, have called for laws mandating the death penalty for homosexuals and drunkards.[26]

Rushdoony's views may be frightening to many secularists and members of the Jewish, Moslem, and Buddhist faiths, but his views are also at odds with premillennialist and amillennialist Christian thought. Unfortunately, *Newsweek* has labeled Rushdoony's Chalcedon Foundation as the think tank of the Religious Right.[27] Indeed, confusion abounds. Rushdoony and his compatriots are regular guests on religious television and radio shows and have won a number of adherents among the charismatics, despite their ardent Calvinism. The books of Rushdoony and his followers are being published by standard Evangelical publishers, and their works have received approving comments by recognized Evangelical leaders.[28]

The basic tenets of Rushdoony's Reconstructionism are:

1. *Presuppositional apologetics.* This is the belief that the Bible is the only legitimate source of Christian truth and that intellectual appeals to reason are useless apart from the convicting power of the Holy Spirit.[29]

2. *Theonomy.* Following their Puritan forefathers, theonomists argue for the government of society by the rule of biblical law. Some Reconstructionists have gone as far as advocating the eventual abolition of democracy and the imposition of Old Testament animal sacrifices.[30]

3. *Postmillennialism.* As already discussed, this view of eschatology is predominant in their system. They do not view the world as a sinking ship, but rather as one that needs to be commandeered and given direction.

The ultimate application of Rushdoony's Reconstructionism would eliminate pluralism in American society in the name of denying legitimacy to non-Christian beliefs. Ironically, many of those who claim to hold democracy so dear have found a temporary ally in one who is inherently opposed to democracy and pluralism.

Amillennialism and the Democratic Process

The history of amillennialism as a precise eschatological view is difficult to trace. It is generally accepted that Augustine of Hippo first articulated this view by arguing that the millennium was to be interpreted allegorically as referring to the church in which Christ reigned in His saints.[31] While this view was challenged in the medieval church by men such as Joachim of Fiore, it remained the dominant view until the time of the Protestant Reformation. Both Luther and Calvin were suspicious of millennial speculation but their followers were not.[32]

Amillennialism has several unique features. Since it views the church as the kingdom of Christ on earth, its adherents are not looking for the coming of the kingdom as are premillennialists, and they are not trying to bring in the kingdom as are postmillennialists. Rather, they believe the kingdom is already present in the church on earth. Therefore, amillennialists are very committed to expressing the character of Christ to the secular world by influencing the political process.

In American politics, amillennialists have generally been very supportive of democratic pluralism. They believe that Christians are to be the spiritual "salt of the earth" within that process. As such they see their role as that of attracting nonbelievers to the truth by exemplary lifestyles. Thus, the believer best influences society by being a true Christian in all his dealings with society.

Amillennialism is the predominant eschatology of today's Presbyterians, Lutherans, and Methodists. It is also held by religious groups as divergent as Catholics and Baptists. In general, amillennialists view the present Church Age as the time when Christ is ruling His kingdom on earth in the lives of true believers.

The present era, they believe, will end with the return of Christ to judge the world, probably including a literal Armageddon, and usher in eternity. According to this eschatological scheme, believers go right from the present world into a heavenly eternity. Amillennialism does not look forward to a millennial reign of Christ on earth. Therefore, its adherents do not look for a Jewish kingdom in which Christ will literally rule the earth from the throne of David in Jerusalem. Thus, the amillennialists' attention is on the church's role *in* society.

Dispensational Premillennialism and the Rapture

The overwhelming majority of Evangelicals and fundamentalists would describe themselves as premillennialists. Actually, they would say they are premillennial dispensationalists. Dispensationalism refers to an eschatological perspective that sees history as a series of "dispensations," or ages, with Christ's return coming at the end. The major fundamentalist seminaries and many televangelists hold this position. Their views have often been criticized as relying on the rapture as the "great escape."

Premillennial dispensationalism was propagated in the nineteenth century by the Plymouth Brethren movement in England. John Nelson Darby (1800–1882) was its most prominent spokesman. It spread to the United States, where the Bible Conference movement brought it into hundreds of thousands of homes.[33] The popular Scofield Reference Bible of the Reverend C.I. Scofield contained extensive notes about dispensationalism.[34] Premillennial dispensationalists tend to identify the final dispensation—the Age of Apostasy—with the rise of theological liberalism in the twentieth century.

Premillennialists believe that the end times will be harbingered by the rapture, which refers to the literal taking up of Christians into heaven. By Christians, they do not mean all professing Christians; rather, only those who have accepted Jesus Christ as their personal Savior. The rapture is suggested by several biblical passages, notably Saint Paul's First Letter to the Thessalonians, in which he says, "For the Lord himself shall descend from heaven with a shout, with the voice of the archangel, and with the trump of God: and the dead in Christ shall rise first: then we which are alive and remain shall be caught up together with them in the clouds, to meet the Lord in the air: and so shall we ever be with the Lord" (1 Thessalonians 4:16,17 KJV).

Popular Evangelical author Tim LaHaye outlines what might ensue after rapture: "The Rapture will be an event of such startling proportions that the entire world will be conscious of our leaving. There will be airplane, bus and train wrecks throughout the world. Who can imagine the chaos on the freeways when automobile drivers are snatched out of their cars? One cannot help surmise that many strangers will be in churches the first Sunday after the rapture. Liberal churches, where heretics in clerical garb have not preached the Word of God, may be filled to capacity with wondering and frantic church members."[35]

Most premillennialists think that the tribulation will follow the rapture. The main reason is that Christian churches are never referred to in the Bible after its account of the rapture. The Bible says that Christians as a force for good will simply be removed from the world, and evil will run rampant. This will correspond with the rise of a force for evil such as the world has never seen before—the Antichrist. In a pamphlet on Armageddon theology, one theologian notes that all the world's dictators—Genghis Khan, Attila the Hun, Hitler, Stalin—acted in the spirit of the Antichrist but could not rival his supreme evil. Evangelicals believe that the Antichrist will make the tyrants of the past seem benign by comparison.

The main target of the Antichrist's fury will be Israel.[36] Dispensationalists believe that the tribulation will largely consist of the Antichrist persecuting the Jews. This, they believe, will be "the time of Jacob's trouble" referred to in

Scripture.[37] Many people also believe that Russia will form an alliance with various Arab countries and eventually invade Israel.[38]

Dispensationalist theologian Dwight Pentecost of Dallas Theological Seminary has said that "God's purpose for Israel in this Tribulation is to bring about the conversion of a multitude of Jews, who will enter into the blessings of the Kingdom and experience the fulfillment of all Israel's covenants."[39] He views the tribulation as ending with the conversion of Israel and the total defeat of the forces of Russia and the Antichrist. Following this will be a literal 1,000-year reign of Christ on earth preceding the last judgment.

Ever since the early part of the twentieth century, premillennial Evangelicals have tended to view the end of the world as imminent. Consequently, they have withdrawn themselves from the institutions of society, regarding political and social reform as futile. They have focused their efforts on evangelistic attempts to win converts to Christ. Some of the more extreme fundamentalists have virtually given up on the world. Their eschatology has made them complacent about such issues as nuclear proliferation, peace in the Middle East, or any attempts to resolve international conflict. Theirs is a dispensationalist fatalism of the worst sort.

Eschatological Realism

Apocalyptic eschatological speculation is certainly a dangerous business because it has dangerous implications when applied to political and social structures. One had better be certain he is right before proceeding too far with his vision for the end. Despite the problems, there is much that is valuable in the eschatological enterprise. Despite their differences, every school of eschatological thought points to the eventual triumph of Christ over the forces of evil. The tough questions are *when* and *how*.

One of the apparently more successful eschatological speculators was the amazing Harry Rimmer.[40] His books, *The Shadow of Coming Events* and *The Coming War and the Rise of Russia*, were written in the 1940s during World War II. Taking Ezekiel's prophecies as his guide, Rimmer forecast early during the war that the Axis powers would lose, that Italy would lose her colonial holdings in North Africa, including Libya and Ethiopia, and that Russia would emerge from the war as the major enemy of Israel and the West. He said this at a time when the Soviet Union was an ally to the United States and Roosevelt was posing amicably with Stalin. Naturally, Rimmer's standing in the Evangelical community rose tremendously after his interpretation proved correct.

Unlike the foretellers of the medieval age, Evangelicals today do not juggle with biblical numbers to come up with dates. Rather, they follow a literal understanding of Scripture, which is very consistent with their general biblical hermeneutic. Perhaps the keystone prophecy that confirms their conviction that these are the end times is the return of the Jews to their ancestral homeland. This is unequivocally forecast in the Bible.[41]

"When Israel was founded in 1948," writes Hal Lindsey in *The Late Great Planet Earth*, "the prophetic countdown began."[42] Many Christians believe that Israel's capture of Old Jerusalem in 1967 is also very significant because it makes possible the rebuilding of the holy temple in Jerusalem. They believe that this is a key biblical sign preceding the second coming. Many Christians interpret Christ's forecast about the end times—"this generation shall not pass, till all these things be fulfilled" (Matthew 24:34 KJV)—as referring to the generation that comes after the founding of Israel; in other words, our generation.[43]

Of course, it is theoretically possible that the Jews will once again be driven from Israel and return at some point in the future to participate in the end-times drama. But common sense dictates that this is very unlikely. Both Jews and Gentiles, both Christians and secularists, agree and recognize that the formation of the state of Israel is an event of the greatest importance. After some 2,000 years of exclusion, the Jews repossess their God-given home. Many believe this to be precursor for the end of the age.

Recently, there has been a considerable segment of the secular community who agree that we are approaching the end of the world. Several Nobel laureates and reputable scientists tell us that the earth's clock may be running low. We hear so much about the possibility of nuclear holocaust and extinction—the very gloomy and apocalyptic vision of Jonathan Schell's *The Fate of the Earth,* for example. When Evangelicals predicted the end of the world in earlier centuries, people laughed at them because the destruction of the entire planet was simply inconceivable. But today it is well within the realm of possibility. In fact, some secularists seem far more worried about it than believers are. They are not, however, accused of trying to hasten the end; indeed, they are often credited with the moral vision that is needed to forestall such an outcome.

Christians also recognize that Scripture says no one knows when the end will come. Jesus Himself said: "No one knows about that day or hour, not even the angels in heaven, nor the Son, but only the Father" (Matthew 24:36). Saint Paul writes of the end, "Now, brothers, about times and dates we do not need to write to you, for you know very well that the day of the Lord will come like a thief in the night" (1 Thessalonians 5:1,2).[44] It is foolish to act according to timetables when God advises against it. Fortunately, having learned from the errors of the past, fewer and fewer Evangelical pastors are doing this.

Christian Responsibility

Just as there are many Bible passages that describe the end times, there are scores of passages that outline Christian responsibilities in this world. We must take both sets of passages seriously. The Bible says that we should be ready for the second coming *and* that we should be good citizens—the salt of the earth. These missions are not contradictory or mutually exclusive. We must work to better the world because the Bible tells us to, and we must await Christ's return because the Scripture commands us to do so. In Luke 19:13, Jesus told His disciples to "occupy" (KJV) or "work" (NIV) until He returns. He meant that we are to be busy about His work, not merely occupying a seat.[45]

This is why Evangelicals and fundamentalists are investing so heavily in the future. All the major conservative Christian groups are building churches and schools and setting up missionary outposts abroad. Most have plans that already go into the twenty-first century. We would not make these plans if we were sure the world would soon be destroyed.

Most Evangelicals are in the arena of politics today to improve secular society, not abandon it. They are working hard to stop abortion, to improve the public schools, and to eliminate pornography. Most of us believe that it is our mandate from God to help make the world a better place to live and to use Christianity as a force for good in this world. We are advocating positive change. We believe life is a gift from God and that it is our duty to protect it. Our involvement clearly indicates that we are not among those whose apocalyptic views are a pretext for this-world despair.

While Christians may disagree among themselves on their views of eschatology and on the proper political response based upon them, one thing is clear: We are getting closer to the end with every day that passes. The time will soon come when all other options will fail. A global holocaust is inevitable.

A Time to Repent

Belief in Armageddon does not mean that we want to hasten its coming. A lot of the talk about speeding up the apocalypse would be stopped if more people understood that prophecy cannot be altered, although there are some conditional prophecies. In the Old Testament, for example, when people repented for their sins God would abstain from sending a divine punishment. But the prophecies about the end times are unconditional. It is arrogant and sinful to think that we can change them. Pat Robertson has said that Armageddon is "an act of God Almighty that has nothing to do with human abilities whatsoever. I have no intention of helping God along in this respect."[46]

The only appropriate response to these prophecies is to repent of our sins and try to bring as many people as possible to Christ. Our political concerns can never diminish the ultimate priority of evangelism. Jesus told His disciples, "Go ye into all the world, and preach the gospel to every creature" (Mark 16:15 KJV). He further added that "repentance and forgiveness of sins will be preached in his name to all nations . . . " (Luke 24:47).

The great commission of our Lord to make disciples of all nations does not promote coerced conversion. Rather, it clearly implies a voluntary acceptance of Christ as Savior and Lord. Even in these last days as we await His return, our biblical obligation is not to bring all people to Christ, but to bring Christ to all people. And for the first time in history, we have the means to do it.

12

Is There
Any Hope?

*"Not by might nor by power, but by
my Spirit," says the LORD Almighty.*
—Zechariah 4:6

The stage is set for the final fulfillment of biblical prophecy. Israel is back in her land after a 2,000-year absence. The European Union is coming together on the continent after 16 centuries of division. The United States, the most powerful nation in the world, seems ready to join forces with the new global community.

The timing of the last days is in God's hands, but from a human standpoint it appears that we are standing on the threshold of the final frontier. The pieces of the puzzle are all in place. As the sands of time slip through the hourglass of eternity, we are all moving closer to an appointment with destiny. The only question is, How much time is left?

The tension between living for today and looking for tomorrow is one of the realities of the Christian life. We often find ourselves caught between the here-and-now and the hereafter. On the one hand, we need to be ready for Jesus to come at any moment. On the other hand, we have God-given responsibilities to fulfill in this world in the meantime.

Personal preparation for Christ's return is a decision each one of us must make. In our Lord's final instructions to His disciples, He said we were to serve as witnesses for Him (Acts 1:8) and evangelize the whole world (Matthew 28:19,20). His plan could not be more clear. He gave no exceptions. He told us exactly what to do until He returned.

What Can We Expect?

Speculating about the future beyond what the Bible itself predicts is a dangerous game. Biblical prophecies give us a clear picture of what to expect in the years ahead:

- The spread of the gospel and *growth of the church* through worldwide evangelism of all nations (Matthew 24:14).

- The rise of *religious apostasy* in the last days, leading to widespread sin and lawlessness (2 Thessalonians 2:3).

- The *rapture of the church* (true believers) to heaven prior to the great tribulation judgments (Revelation 3:10).

- The rise of the *Antichrist* and the *False Prophet* to control the new world order of the end times (Revelation 13:1-4,11-18).

- The **tribulation period** on earth with widespread ecological destruction, war, and famine (Matthew 24:21,22).

- The **triumphal return** of Christ with His church to overthrow the Antichrist and bind Satan for 1,000 years (Revelation 19:11-16; 20:1,2).

Beyond these key events, we can only speculate about what will happen in the future. The Bible predicts an age of unparalleled selfism in the last days (2 Timothy 3:1-6). It also predicts an age of skepticism and unbelief—a time when people will scoff at the idea of Christ's return (2 Peter 3:3,4). It also appears that this age will be marked by global wealth and prosperity (Revelation 18:11-19).

The next generation could well be the last one on planet Earth. All indications are that the years ahead will be marked by widespread production of nuclear bombs by third-world nations, some of which are led by trigger-happy, egotistical dictators. All of this is happening in the midst of the continued deterioration of the earth's atmosphere and environment.

What Can We Do?

It has often been said "there is no panic in heaven, only plans." God is still on the throne of the universe, and nothing is beyond the control of His sovereign will. Therefore, we do not need to panic, nor should we be complacent. There is much God is calling us to do in light of the return of Christ. Here is a suggested list:

1. **Evangelize the world** with the gospel ("good news") of Christ's love (Matthew 28:19,20).

2. *Infiltrate every walk of life* as the "salt of the earth" and let your *spiritual light shine* by the sincerity and integrity of your Christian life (Matthew 5:13-16).

3. *Speak out* as the voice of Christ to the needs of society even if it costs you (Matthew 5:11,12.)

Since we do not know when the rapture will occur, we can never assume God's purposes for His church are finalized. We must remain obedient to Christ's commands until the trumpet sounds. Jesus told the disciples, "It is not for you to know the times or dates the Father has set by his own authority" (Acts 1:7). It is clear from this statement that the date has been set by God, and we aren't supposed to know it because we have a responsibility to fulfill in the meantime.

In the very next verse, Jesus gave the great commission, telling His disciples to be His witnesses "to the ends of the earth" (Acts 1:8). We are to evangelize the world until Jesus calls us home to heaven. God never reveals the date to us because He knows all too well we wouldn't take His commission seriously until we were about to run out of time.

Can We Make a Difference?

We are faced with a great dilemma at the dawn of the new millennium. We are confronted with choices forced upon us by our materialistic and technologically advanced society. We must decide between comfort and commitment. We must ask ourselves if we are willing to pay the price for freedom and justice before it is too late. Will we give all that we have to reach this world for Christ or will we take all we can for ourselves? The choice is ours!

Christians of past generations were much more committed than most believers are today. They often forsook the comforts of home to invest their lives in helping others. Many risked their very lives to reach a lost world with the gospel of hope in Jesus Christ. At the end of his life, the great missionary statesman David Livingstone remarked that all that he lost was worth it in light of eternity.

William Willimon, chaplain of Duke University, has raised the issue of political neutrality in relation to what he calls the "chains of religious freedom."[1] He argues that a purely secularized democracy offers us religious freedom only so far as we are willing to keep our public mouths shut. He writes, "We enjoy freedom to be Jewish or Christian here as long as we keep our religion to ourselves and let the government handle public matters." He goes on to argue that the church must be willing to speak out against moral wrong whether our message offends the secular mind-set or not.

"Observers of our national moral decay call for a restored religious underpinning of our national ideals," Willimon adds. "At the same time they want the state to be 'completely neutral.' But how would Christians set out to provide moral underpinning apart from their commitment to Jesus Christ, which can hardly be described as neutral?"[2]

The time has come for Evangelicals to speak as messengers of God to the great evils of our society. We cannot keep quiet on the flimsy excuse that we don't want to appear excessive or hypocritical. Our agenda must be refined in light of the moral and political debate. We must prioritize that agenda to give the greatest attention to the greatest needs.

The Naked Public Square

In many ways politics has become our last line of defense against the legal enshrinement of raw secularism.

It is no secret that American society has become increasingly secularized throughout the twentieth century. As secularism gained an ever-increasing grip on the intellectual life of America, it should have been obvious that it would eventually seek to impose its beliefs by political legislation. Thus, in this process, politics becomes the final expression of the beliefs of those involved. Just as the founders of America sought to give politics a religious and moral vision, so the secularizers of America have sought to give it a secular vision.[3]

R.C. Sproul has rightly observed, "Students of history realize that no society can survive, no civilization can function, without some unifying system of thought."[4] This unifying system generally takes the form of a philosophy, religion, myth, or political system to which society becomes devoted. America has always been an unusual combination of both a religious and political system ever since the pilgrims on the *Mayflower* came to America "for the Glory of God and the advancement of the Christian faith."

British historian Paul Johnson has observed, "The political culture of the United States is strongly religious" because of the "harmony of religion and liberty." He explains that religion has always been the champion of liberty in America and, therefore, there is no conflict between the religious establishment and the political process. Indeed, he argues that the influence of religion in America can be traced back to Puritans like Jonathan Edwards, who saw religion as the unifying force in American society."[5]

Richard Neuhaus has argued very effectively that religion and democracy can indeed coexist. However, he observes that the current trend in American society toward overt secularization leaves the square of public policy naked of the very values upon which it was established. "To be truly democratic and to endure," he writes, "such a public policy must be grounded in values that are based in Judeo-Christian religion."[6] He argues that Evangelicals have foolishly avoided social and political involvement, naïvely assuming that someone else would shape public policy in their best interests. "Attention must be paid to the political," Neuhaus asserts, "not because everything is political, but because, if attention is not paid, the political threatens to encompass everything."[7]

This is the problem that brought Evangelicals into politics in the first place. The vast majority of them have never called for the establishment of a theocracy. Most of them are not even calling for a reconstruction of the American legal system. They simply want the secularists to leave the system alone. But in the meantime, they do not intend to sit idly by and watch secularists reconstruct America into an antireligious state.

Evangelical Christians believe that American public policy should reflect our nation's biblical and moral heritage. If it does not, most Evangelicals hope that at least it will not undermine that legacy. In other words, when a political or judicial decision is made that reflects antireligious beliefs, Evangelicals take it as a personal affront to their beliefs. It is only natural that they would react against such policies.

Neuhaus also has observed that Evangelicals have often been guilty of perpetuating the naked public square by refusing to enter the public policy debate. Thus, Neuhaus argues, the separation of private belief from public policy actually allows secularism to spread unchecked.[8] We cannot have a moral society and a value-free society at the same time. In other words, as secularism prevails in a society, traditional values begin to disappear.

The Bankruptcy of Liberalism

One of the major problems in American religion has been the nearly total capitulation of liberal mainline religion to the secular agenda. In what Neuhaus calls the "Great Accommodation," the prophets of liberalism became pacifiers of secularism and left religion "bereft of its miraculous and transcendent quality."[9]

Unfortunately, the popular reception of the social gospel by the mainline churches shifted their emphasis from evangelism to social concern. In time, the liberal wing of the church allied itself almost totally with left-wing political stances. In reaction to both the liberal theology and liberal politics of the mainline churches, fundamentalists and Evangelicals shifted more dramatically toward the right. Eventually, the two camps of American Protestantism became polarized on virtually every issue.

Like the hare racing the tortoise, the mainline churches falsely assumed that they had the race won, and they began to rest on their laurels. However, they were lacking a crucial ingredient, which was a reflection of their defective theology—evangelism! They made no effort to win new converts to their beliefs. As a result, they began to decline numerically. Today that decline has become a toboggan slide to oblivion. At the rate the mainline churches are losing members, they are in danger of eventually going out of existence.[10]

This calamity contains a somber warning to conservative Christians. We could also be in danger of hitching our theology to a particular political position that could result more in the politicizing of Christianity than in the Christianizing of politics. Charles Colson has warned: "Today's misspent enthusiasm for political solutions to the moral problems of our culture arises from . . . too low a view of the power of a sovereign God and too high a view of the ability of man."[11]

Phenomenal Growth of Evangelical Churches

The term *Evangelical* is derived from the word *evangel* ("gospel" or "good news"). The evangelistic proclamation of the gospel is the cornerstone of the Evangelical church. *Evangelical* encompasses a wide range of conservative Christians. While great differences of theology, ministry, and worship exist among various types of Evangelicals, they are all committed to sharing the gospel. In their own way and style, each subgroup of Evangelicals are winning millions of converts to Christ from America's unchurched population and from within the ranks of the mainline churches.

The years of socio-political involvement for Evangelicals have not been easy ones. Early victories, self-proclaimed successes, and euphoric triumphalism have given way to a more serious assessment of the reality of long-term political involvement. It is to be hoped that we have now realized there are no shortcuts to success and no simple solutions to our national problems. Future endeavors are going to need to be carefully weighed and evaluated. Specific priorities for our efforts need to be established in the areas where we can do the most good.

By now, we should also have learned that we can make a difference in the public policy formation of this country if we will be patient with the democratic process. We may not be able to change things overnight, but we have gotten the attention of the nation. No longer can politicians simply dismiss Christians as an irrelevant minority. Forty to 50 million professing born-again believers are a sizable portion of the population. We can make our voices heard, and we can make a difference in our national life.

The Compelling Necessity

While there are certainly potential dangers in political involvement, there is also the compelling necessity of our involvement. "Failure to do so," writes Richard Neuhaus, "results in the abandonment of our responsibility to care for the world that is the object of God's creating and preserving love." He argues that culture formation and politics are among the ways in which Christians are called to serve their neighbors.[12]

John Stott adds the compelling analysis that Evangelicals tend to want to drop out of the political process every time the going gets rough. He blames this on two factors. First, he argues that many Christians have such an other-worldly orientation that they become indifferent to social injustice as long as it doesn't affect them personally. These "irresponsible escapists," as he calls them, are the modern equivalent of ancient mystics pietistically hiding in monasteries while the rest of the world is in chaos. Second, he accuses some American Evangelicals of being so success-oriented that they bail out of every cause they think they can't win."[13]

The ultimate mission of the church is above political parties and personalities. Thus, the church must never become so entangled in the political process that it cannot objectively criticize and confront it. But neither can the church exist in a hermetically sealed environment where it is conveniently divorced from the political process by a self-imposed monasticism.

Throughout church history, five basic church and society models have been proposed.[14]

1. ***Isolation.*** This approach advocates a total or near-total isolation of Christians from society. It urges believers to live in relation to God alone, and it isolates the church from any social or political action. Pietistic evangelicalism has a tendency in this direction. It adopts the attitude, "Our ministry is spiritual. If we forget about the world, it won't bother us."

2. ***Accommodation.*** This approach encourages the church to accommodate itself to society in order to influence it. This has been the general approach of Protestant liberalism. On the one hand, it avoids the extreme of isolation, but on the other hand, it generally succumbs to a capitulation of its values to those of the secular society.

3. ***Condemnation.*** This is the position of many militant fundamentalists, who are quick to condemn the ills of society while offering little or nothing to correct them. They know what they don't like, but they are never really clear about what to do about it. While many aspects of society need to be confronted by the church, society also needs the opportunity to establish proper alternatives which are biblically based.

4. ***Integration.*** According to this approach, there is always a tension between the church and society, which reflects what Luther called the "eschatological struggle between the power of God and the powers of evil."[15] In this model, which has generally

been adopted by the Evangelical community, the Christian has a constructive role to play in society. Therefore, he may influence society by his presence, but he generally does so with little or no intention of changing society by social or political action.

5. *Transformation.* This is the model developed by John Calvin, who believed God was sovereign both over the church and the state. He saw the church as involved in the ceaseless activity of bringing order out of chaos. In the political realm, this means transforming society by the authority of Scripture and under the claims of the Lordship of Christ. He wrote that government should "adopt our conduct to human society, to form our manners to civil justice, to conciliate us to each other, and to cherish common peace and tranquility."[16] He viewed public magistrates as ordained servants of God to protect innocence, modesty, honor, and tranquility.

Biblical prophecies about the rise of the Antichrist clearly indicate that he will not be fully revealed until after the rapture. If this is true, we must not give up our Lord's command to evangelize the world with the gospel (Matthew 28:19,20). We dare not abandon our society to the evil one without a fight.

Tim LaHaye argues that Evangelicals are making a substantial difference in our society. LaHaye recently said, "One lesson we've learned . . . is that if we give into the pacifism that has been our tradition since the pietistic movement, we will be steam-rolled by the secular-humanist juggernaut that is determined to secularize public policy."[17]

The church has been given a spiritual mandate in this world. We are to live our lives uniquely committed to God. At the same time, we must live out our spiritual commitment in today's society. Since our God is a moral being, we cannot divorce spirituality from morality. In the context of a free democratic society, we can and should work to see the principles of God exonerated in our society.

We may not win the battle in the immediate future. And we certainly won't win it in the end. Eventually, the waves of secularism, humanism and relativism will erode much of what is still truly Christian in our society, paving the way for the rise of the Antichrist to power. In the meantime, we have a God-given mandate to oppose the powers of evil until the trumpet sounds and God calls the church home to heaven.

Satan's Final Defeat

The ultimate victory of Christ began with His incarnation. When Jesus was born, God entered the human arena in a physical body (see John 1:14). Jesus looked like a man but He talked like God. He lived among man but He lived above man. His initial triumph came in His victory over temptation (Matthew 4:1-11). He faced Satan on his own turf and was overwhelmingly victorious.

In the meantime, Jesus continued to display His divine power over Satan by healing the sick, raising the dead, and casting out demons. Michael Green observes, "Throughout his ministry Jesus cast out demons and drove back the power of the enemy in the lives of those who came to trust in him."[18] Thus, our Lord's entire earthly ministry was a foretaste of victory to come.

The climax came on the cross. Instead of the crucifixion becoming a defeat, it became the turning point in
the whole war. There, Jesus triumphed over sin and death.
He took the punishment of God's wrath for our sins by
nailing them to the cross. He triumphed over the accuser so
that there is "no condemnation for those who are in Christ
Jesus" (Romans 8:1).

There is a long-standing tradition in Christianity that
the death of Christ constituted what Michael Green calls
"the harrowing of hell."[19] First Peter 3:18-22 makes it clear
that "Christ died for sins once for all, the righteous for the
unrighteous, to bring you to God." Then Peter notes that
Jesus descended into hell to announce His triumph in
Satan's lair. This announcement (Greek, *ekeruxeni)* is not
an evangelistic appeal but a statement of finality. Green
adds, "This means that he heralded his victory over all the
powers of evil with such cosmic significance that this news
percolated into the depths of hell's innermost dungeon."[20]

Satan is a defeated foe! Ever since that "first mouthful
of dust" in Eden, writes Donald Grey Barnhouse, "Satan
has been left with a scrambled world which he has been
unable to organize, but which lay a wreck and a ruin,
beneath the darkness of God's judgment."[21] The dark one
cannot bring light to the world. The father of lies cannot
emancipate the creation with truth. Satan cannot create,
he can only destroy. "The resulting disorder is the chaos of
history," notes Barnhouse.[22]

God has allowed Satan and his demonic and human
cohorts to run this world within the limits of His divine
permission, and the resulting chaos testifies against them!
Even Satan's "masterpiece," the Antichrist, unwittingly
serves the purposes of God in bringing mankind to the
brink of destruction. Erwin Lutzer has observed that if the

devil exists by God's permission, then the devil is God's devil and the Antichrist is His servant.[23]

Satan's ultimate humiliation will come at the battle of Armageddon (Revelation 16:16; 19:11–20:2). There, all the forces of evil will be defeated by the triumphal return of Christ. The beast and the False Prophet will be cast into the lake of fire, and Satan will be chained in the abyss for 1,000 years. Then, after his final rebellion, Satan himself will be cast into the lake of fire (Revelation 20:10).

The *judgment of Satan* will then be complete. He will have been:

1. forbidden access to Eden (Genesis 3:14,24).

2. forbidden to reside in heaven (Revelation 12:7-12).

3. forbidden to dwell on earth (Revelation 20:2,3).

4. cast into the lake of fire (Revelation 20:10).

What shall we say then of the evil one? His powers are limited. His defeat is certain. His destruction is imminent. And his "masterpiece"? The Antichrist's rule will be limited. His reign destructive. His power annihilated. And his doom will be permanent.

Yes, the "spirit of the Antichrist" is already at work in the world. Satan's strategy is formulated against Christ. He is waiting for the right moment in time to indwell the one who will become the beast. Even now, he could be alive and well on planet Earth. He could be rising to power somewhere in the Western world, promising peace and offering hope for the world's great problems. But something is holding him back. He cannot be revealed until the restraining influence of the church is removed at the rapture. Then all hell will break loose and the deceiver will rise to power (2 Thessalonians 2:3-12).

In the meantime, we need not fear the arrival of the beast. He cannot begin his diabolical work until our task of world evangelization is finished (Matthew 24:14). Jesus has commanded us to go into all the world with the good news of God's grace until the body of Christ is complete, and He calls us home to be with Him.

Oh, what a day that will be! The Lord Jesus will descend from heaven; rapture His bride, the church; judge the world; win the battle of Armageddon; defeat the Antichrist; bind Satan; and set up His kingdom on earth. In light of eternity, every heartache of earth will fade away. It is no wonder the church has always said, "Even so, come Lord Jesus!"

Notes

Chapter 1: The Coming World Ruler

1. Ed Dobson, *The End* (Grand Rapids: Zondervan, 1997), pp. 97-98. This fascinating and insightful study of end-time prophecies discusses the "Rise and Fall of the Antichrist" in detail on pp. 97-110.

2. Gregory Boyd, *God at War: Bible and Spiritual Conflict* (Downers Grove, IL: InterVarsity Press, 1997), p. 11.

3. Grant Jeffrey, *Prince of Darkness* (Toronto: Frontier Research Publications, 1994), pp. 48-55.

4. Quoted by Jeffrey, Ibid., p. 53.

5. Richard Trench, *Synonyms of the New Testament* (Grand Rapids: Eerdmans, n.d.), p. 107.

6. Cf. Charles Feinberg, *Daniel*, (Chappaqua, New York: Christian Herald Books, 1981); Robert Culver, *Daniel and the Latter Days* (Chicago: Moody Press, 1954); Stephen Miller, *Daniel: New American Commentary*, vol. 18 (Nashville: Broadman & Holman, 1994); John Walvoord, *Daniel: Key to Prophetic Revelation* (Chicago: Moody Press, 1971); John Whitcomb, *Daniel* (Chicago: Moody Press, 1985).

7. Stephen Miller, *Daniel: New American Commentary*, vol. 18 (Nashville: Broadman & Holman, 1994), p. 307.

8. Charles Feinberg, *Daniel* (Chappaqua, New York: Christian Herald Books, 1981), pp. 174-175.

9. Arno Froese, *How Democracy Will Elect the Antichrist* (Columbia, SC: The Olive Press, 1997), pp. 113, 138-39.

10. Harvey Cox, *The Seduction of the Spirit* (New York: Simon & Schuster, 1973), p. 16. See also Ed Dobson and Ed Hindson, *The Seduction of Power* (Old Tappan, NJ: Revell, 1988).

11. Arthur W. Pink, *The Antichrist* (Minneapolis: Klock & Klock, 1979), p. 77.

12. Jeffrey, *Prince*, pp. 29-30; see also Pink, *Antichrist*, pp. 83-88.

Chapter 2: The Ultimate Deception

1. J. Dwight Pentecost, *Things to Come* (Grand Rapids: Zondervan, 1965), p. 339.
2. See Mal Couch, ed. , *Dictionary of Premillennial Theology* (Grand Rapids: Kregel, 1996), p. 117.
3. Thomas Ice and Timothy Demy, *Fast Facts on Bible Prophecy* (Eugene, OR: Harvest House, 1997), p. 77.
4. Ibid., pp. 78-79.
5. Samuel Andrews, *Christianity and Anti-Christianity* (Chicago: Moody Bible Institute, 1898), p. 320.
6. John F. Walvoord, *Major Bible Prophecies* (Grand Rapids: Zondervan, 1991), p. 324.
7. Walter K. Price, *The Coming Antichrist* (Chicago: Moody Press, 1974), p. 162.
8. Ibid.
9. John Owen, *Apostasy from the Gospel,* abridged by R.J.K. Law (Edinburgh: Banner of Truth, 1992), p. 135.
10. Ibid.
11. Ibid., pp. 148-50.
12. Herman Hoyt, *The End Times* (Chicago: Moody Press, 1969), p. 129. Cf. Dave Hunt, *A Woman Rides the Beast* (Eugene, OR: Harvest House, 1994).
13. Frank Mankiewicz and Joel Swerdlow, *Remote Control: Television and the Manipulation of American Life* (New York: Ballantine Books, 1978), p. i.
14. Ibid., p. 7; see also Tal Brooke, *Virtual Gods* (Eugene, OR: Harvest House, 1997).
15. Mankiewicz and Swerdlow, *Remote Control,* page 6.
16. Ibid., pp. 5-11.
17. Quoted in ibid., p. 5.
18. E.B. White, *The New Yorker* (1938), quoted by Mankiewicz and Swerdlow, *Remote Control,* facing page of Preface.
19. Ibid.
20. Harvey Cox, *The Seduction of the Spirit* (New York: Simon & Schuster, 1973), p. 303.
21. Ibid., p. 305.

Chapter 3: Rise of False Prophets

1. A.T. Pierson, *The Bible and Spiritual Life* (Fincastle, VA: Scripture Truth, reprint of 1887 Exeter Hall lectures), p. 169.
2. C.S. Lewis, *Mere Christianity* (New York: MacMillan, 1960), pp. 53-54.
3. Mary Baker Eddy, *Science and Health with Key to the Scriptures* (Boston: Trustees, 1925), p. 150.

4. Ibid., pp. vii-viii.
5. Hank Hanegraaff, *Christianity in Crisis* (Eugene, OR: Harvest House, 1993).
6. "Children of the Apocalypse," *Newsweek* (May 3, 1993), p. 30.
7. Alan Bloom, *The Closing of the American Mind* (New York: Simon & Schuster, 1986), pp. 25-85.
8. Ibid., p. 34.
9. Ibid., pp. 82-85.
10. Harold Bussell, *Unholy Devotion: Why Cults Lure Christians* (Grand Rapids, MI: Zondervan, 1983), pp. 61-72.
11. David Breese, *The Marks of a Cult* (Eugene, OR: Harvest House, 1998).
12. Ibid., p. 51.
13. Christopher Edwards, *Crazy for God* (Englewood Cliffs, NJ: Prentice-Hall, 1979), p. 200.
14. Elliot Miller, *A Crash Course in the New Age Movement* (Grand Rapids: Baker, 1989), pp. 17-18.

Chapter 4: The Darkness of Our Times

1. Quoted by Charles Colson, *Against the Night* (Ann Arbor, MI: Servant, 1989), p. 55.
2. Ibid., pp. 133-34.
3. 2 Thessalonians 2:3.
4. Peter Lalonde, *One World Under Antichrist* (Eugene, OR: Harvest House, 1991), p. 58.
5. Barbara Marx Hubbard, *The Book of Co-Creation: An Evolutionary Interpretation of the New Testament,* unpublished manuscript dated 1980. Quoted by Lalonde, *One World,* pp. 166-67.
6. Lalonde, *One World,* p. 173.
7. Michael Horton, ed. , *The Agony of Deceit* (Chicago: Moody Press, 1990).
8. Marvin Stone, "What Kind of People Are We?" *U.S. News & World Report* (February 5, 1979).
9. Francis Schaeffer and C. Everett Koop, M.D., *Whatever Happened to the Human Race?* (Old Tappan, NJ: Revell, 1979), p. 89.
10. Charles Wesley, "And Can It Be That I Should Gain," *Hymns of the Living Church* (Carol Stream, IL: Hope Publishing Co., 1974), no. 248.

Chapter 5: Dawn of the New Millennium

1. Paul Johnson, *Modern Times: The World from the Twenties to the Eighties* (San Francisco: Harper & Row, 1983). A perceptive treatment of current trends by the eminent British historian.
2. See the development of this theme in Francis Schaeffer, *How Should We Then Live?* (Old Tappan, NJ: Revell, 1976), pp. 130-66.

3. This issue is discussed by a variety of Evangelical writers. See R.C. Sproul, *Lifeviews*, pp. 113-27; Richard Neuhaus, *The Naked Public Square*, pp. 94-143; Carl F.H. Henry, *Christian Countermoves in a Decadent Culture* (Portland: Multnomah Press, 1986), pp. 31-46; Francis Schaeffer, *The Great Evangelical Disaster* (Westchester, IL: Crossway Books, 1984), pp. 111-46.

4. For a brilliant assessment of this method of thinking and its influence on religion, see Harry Blamires, *The Christian Mind* (Ann Arbor, MI: Servant Books, 1978), pp. 3-66.

5. Allan Bloom, *The Closing of the American Mind* (New York: Simon & Schuster, 1987). The underlying theme is that higher education has failed democracy and impoverished the souls of today's students.

6. Ibid., p. 19.

7. Ibid., pp. 25-43.

8. Ibid., p. 82.

9. Ibid., p. 85.

10. Arthur Levine, *When Dreams and Heroes Died: A Portrait of Today's College Student* (San Francisco: Jossey-Bass Publishers, 1980). In this study sponsored by the Carnegie Foundation for the Advancement of Teaching, Levine observes that today's students are self-centered, individualistic escapists who want little responsibility for solving society's problems, but who want society to provide them with the opportunity to fulfill their desires.

11. This point is argued strongly by Francis Schaeffer in *The Great Evangelical Disaster*, pp. 141-51. In fact, Schaeffer insists that the disaster among Evangelicals is their accommodation to the spirit of the age, which will lead to "the removal of the last barrier against the breakdown of our culture."

12. Francis Schaeffer and C. Everett Koop, *Whatever Happened to the Human Race?* (Old Tappan, NJ: Revell, 1979).

13. Peter Singer, "Sanctity of Life or Quality of Life," *Pediatrics* (July 1983), pp. 128, 129.

14. Cal Thomas, "Taking the Hypocritical Oath," in *Occupied Territory* (Nashville: Wolgemuth & Hyatt, 1987), pp. 22-24.

15. Stuart Briscoe, *Playing by the Rules* (Old Tappan, NJ: Revell, 1986), pp. 98, 99.

16. Quoted by Tim LaHaye, *The Race for the 21st Century* (Thomas Nelson: Nashville, 1986), p. 135.

17. Ibid., pp. 139-42.

18. Sproul, *Lifeviews* (Old Tappan, NJ: Revell, 1990), p. 62.

19. Quoted in ibid., p. 69.

20. Francis Schaeffer, *A Christian Manifesto* (Westchester, IL: Crossway Books, 1981).

21. For a history of this conflict, see Ed Dobson, Ed Hindson, and Jerry Falwell, *The Fundamentalist Phenomenon* (Garden City, NY: Doubleday, 1981), pp. 47-77.

22. Francis Schaeffer, *Escape from Reason* (Chicago: InterVarsity Press, 1968). This concept is discussed throughout Schaeffer's first book and is presented in a limited diagram on p. 43.

23. Ibid., pp. 43, 44.

24. See Richard J. Newhaus, "Religion: From Privilege to Penalty," *Religion & Society Report* (March 1988), pp. 1, 2.

25. Charles Colson, *Kingdoms in Conflict* (Grand Rapids, MI: Zondervan, 1987), pp. 220-23.

26. Ibid., p. 221.

27. Ibid., p. 221. He quotes James Wall in the *Christian Century* without a specific reference.

28. Ibid., p. 222.

29. Sproul, *Lifeviews*, p. 35.

30. See T.J. Altizer and W. Hamilton, *Radical Theology and the Death of God* (New York: Bobbs-Merrill, 1966). For an Evangelical response, see John W. Montgomery, *The "Is God Dead?" Controversy* (Grand Rapids: Zondervan, 1966).

31. Sproul, *Lifeviews*, p. 37.

32. Truman Dollar, "The Drift Away from Life," *Fundamentalist Journal* (March 1988), p. 58.

33. Os Guinness, *The Dust of Death* (Downers Grove, IL: InterVarsity Press, 1973), pp. 17ff.

34. Ibid., p. 17.

35. Ibid., p. 25.

36. Ibid., pp. 25, 26, quoting Jean Paul Sartre, *Nausea* (Baltimore: Penguin Books, 1965), p. 191.

37. Guinness, ibid., pp. 28,29.

38. Zhores Medvedev, *A Question of Madness* (New York: Alfred Knopf, 1971). See also "Psychoadaptation, or How to Handle Dissenters," *Time* (September 27, 1971), p. 45.

39. Guinness, *Dust*, p. 41.

40. For a general survey of New Age teachings, see the Spiritual Counterfeits Project study by Karen Hoyt, *The New Age Rage* (Old Tappan, NJ: Revell, 1987).

41. Ibid., pp. 21-32.

42. See William Kilpatrick, *The Emperor's New Clothes: The Naked Truth About the New Psychology* (Westchester, IL: Crossway Books, 1985); and Garth Wood, *The Myth of Neurosis* (New York: Harper & Row, 1986).

Chapter 6: Religion of the Future

1. Elliot Miller, *A Crash Course on the New Age Movement* (Grand Rapids: Baker, 1989), p. 24.
2. Ibid., pp. 21-22.
3. Marilyn Ferguson, *The Aquarian Conspiracy* (Los Angeles: J.P. Tarcher, 1980). Her claims may be overstated, but they certainly represent the hopes and dreams of New Age evangelists.
4. Constance Cumbey, *The Hidden Dangers of the Rainbow* (Shreveport, LA: Huntington House, 1983); Miller, *Crash Course*, p. 107.
5. Mark Satin, *New Age Politics* (New York: Dell Books, 1978).
6. Joe Klimo, *Channeling* (Los Angeles: J.P. Tarcher, 1987), p. 185.
7. Sanaya Roman and Duane Packer, *Opening to Channel* (Tiburon, CA: H.J. Kramer, 1987), p. 127.
8. C.S. Lewis, *Screwtape Letters* (London: Collins, 1964), p. 25.
9. Shakti Gawain, *Creative Visualization* (San Rafael, CA: New World Library, 1978), p. 15.
10. Ibid., p. 18.
11. Ibid., pp. 36-40.
12. Miller, *Crash Course*, p. 15.
13. Ibid., p. 16.
14. Fritjof Capra, *The Turning Point* (Toronto: Bantam Books, 1982), p. 302.
15. Miller, *Crash Course*, p. 65.
16. Donald Keys, *Earth at Omega: Passage to Planetization* (Boston: Branden Press, 1982), p. iv.
17. John White, "Channeling: A Short History of a Long Tradition," *Holistic Life* (Summer 1985), p. 20.
18. Cumbey, *Hidden Dangers*, p. 7.

Chapter 7: Globalism and the World Economy

1. John Naisbitt and Pat Aburdene, *Megatrends 2000* (New York: William Morrow, 1990).
2. Robert Reich, *The Work of Nations* (New York: Alfred Knopf, 1992), p. 3.
3. Ibid., p. 113.
4. Quoted by Reich, Ibid., p. 119.
5. Ibid., p. 120.
6. Naisbitt and Aburdene, *Megatrends 2000*, p. 39.
7. Ibid., p. 54.
8. Pat Robertson, *The New World Order* (Dallas: Word, 1991), p. 118. This is probably the finest chapter in Robertson's book.
9. Herbert Schlossberg, *Idols for Destruction* (Nashville: Thomas Nelson, 1983), p. 6.

10. Ibid., p. 1.

Chapter 8: *Future Political Super-State*

1. Helmut Kohl, "This Unity Is Just the Beginning," *The European* (October 11-17, 1991), special report, p. 1.
2. Commonly reported in the press, February 9, 1992.
3. Ibid.
4. Kohl, "This Unity," p. 1.
5. "Charging Ahead," *Time,* (September 18, 1989), p. 45.
6. Malachi Martin, *The Keys of This Blood* (New York: Simon & Schuster, 1990).
7. Ibid., p. 15.
8. See Pat Robertson, *The New World Order* (Dallas: Word, 1991); and Ed Hindson, *End Times, the Middle East and the New World Order* (Chicago: Victor Books, 1991).
9. Larry Burkett, *The Coming Economic Earthquake* (Chicago: Moody Press, 1991).
10. "Charging Ahead," *Time* magazine (September 18, 1989), pp. 40-45.
11. *U.S. News & World Report* (October 15, 1990), p. 64.
12. Arno Froese, *How Democracy Will Elect the Antichrist* (Columbia, SC: The Olive Press, 1997), p. 165.
13. Ibid., p. 172.
14. *The European* (July 6, 1995), p. 17.
15. Froese, *How Democracy*, p. 173.
16. Ibid., p. 200.
17. Ibid., p. 210.
18. See J. Dwight Pentecost, *Things to Come* (Grand Rapids: Zondervan, 1964), pp. 239-50; and Alva McClain, *Daniel's Prophecy of the Seventy Weeks* (Grand Rapids: Zondervan, 1940).
19. Robert Anderson, *The Coming Prince* (London: Hodder & Stoughton, 1909).
20. Froese, *How Democracy,* p. 102.

Chapter 9: *War Is Inevitable!*

1. Adolf Berle, *Power* (New York: Harcourt, Brace & World, 1967), p. 17.
2. Ibid., pp. 37-80.
3. Ibid., p. 37.
4. John Kotter, *Power in Management* (New York: American Management Association, 1979), pp. 13-23.
5. Aleksandr Solzhenitsyn, *A World Split Apart* (New York: Harper & Row, 1978), p. 61.

6. Stephen Budiansky, "The Nuclear Epidemic," *U.S. News & World Report* (March 16, 1992), p. 40.

7. Ibid., pp. 40-44.

8. Carla Anne Robbins, "The X Factor in the Proliferation Game," *U.S. News & World Report* (March 16, 1992), p. 45.

9. Ed Dobson, *The End* (Grand Rapids: Zondervan, 1997), pp. 14ff.

10. Jamie Peterson, ed., *The Aftermath: Human and Ecological Consequences of Nuclear War* (New York: Pantheon Books, 1993), pp. 16-17.

11. Dobson, *The End*, p. 15.

12. Alvin and Heidi Toffler, *War and Anti-War* (Boston: Little, Brown & Co., 1993), p. 3.

13. Ibid., p. 14.

14. Ibid., pp. 247-50.

15. Dobson, *The End*, p. 17.

16. Ibid.

17. J. Dwight Pentecost, *Things to Come* (Grand Rapids: Zondervan, 1965), p. 340.

18. John Walvoord, *Major Bible Prophecies* (New York: Harper Collins, 1991), p. 420.

19. Ibid., p. 422.

20. Thomas Ice and Timothy Demy, *Fast Facts on Bible Prophecy* (Eugene, OR: Harvest House, 1997), p. 24.

21. John Stott, *Involvement: Being a Responsible Christian in a Non-Christian Society* (Old Tappan, NJ: Revell, 1984), vol. 1, p. 31.

22. Richard Neuhaus, "The Post-Secular Task of the Churches," in C.F. Griffith, ed., *Christianity and Politics* (Washington, D.C.: Ethics & Public Policy Center, 1981), pp. 1-18.

Chapter 10: Prophecies of the End Times

1. Quoted at length in Jerry Falwell, *Armageddon* (Wheaton, IL: Tyndale House, 1984), pp. 11ff.

2. C.F. Hogg and W.E. Vine, *The Epistles to the Thessalonians* (London: Exeter Press, 1929), p. 144.

3. Ibid., p. 242.

4. George Milligan, *St. Paul's Epistles to the Thessalonians* (Old Tappan, NJ: Revell, 1988), p. 96.

5. Harold Willmington, *Willmington's Guide to the Bible* (Wheaton, IL: Tyndale House, 1981), p. 833.

6. Ed Dobson, *The End* (Grand Rapids: Zondervan, 1997), pp. 113-14.

7. Desmond Ford, *The Abomination of Desolation in Biblical Eschatology* (Washington, D.C.: University Press of America, 1979), p. 269.

8. Dobson, *The End*, pp. 114-15.

9. Rene Pache, *The Return of Christ* (Chicago: Moody Press, 1955), p. 391.

Chapter 11: How Close Is the End?

1. Hal Lindsey, *The Late Great Planet Earth* (Grand Rapids: Zondervan, 1970).
2. Comment during Reagan–Mondale debates in 1984, as commonly reported in the press.
3. See Ed Dobson and E. Hindson, "Apocalypse Now? What Fundamentalists Believe About the End of the World," in *Policy Review* (Fall 1986), pp. 16-22.
4. This issue is raised by W.S. Lasor in *The Truth About Armageddon* (Grand Rapids: Baker, 1982), pp. 135-49.
5. The Reorganized Church of Jesus Christ of Latter Day Saints still holds to the temple site in Independence, Missouri, which was forsaken by Brigham Young and his followers who later settled in Salt Lake City, Utah.
6. Thomas Goodwin, *A Glimpse of Syons Glory* (London: 1641). For a discussion of Goodwin's position, see Peter Toon, ed., *Puritans, the Millennium and the Future of Israel* (Cambridge: James Clarke, 1970), pp. 64, 65, and Appendix I.
7. See details in Tai Liu, *Discord in Zion: The Puritan Divines and the Puritan Revolution 1640–1660* (The Hague: Martinus Nijhoff, 1973), pp. 1-24.
8. See Earl Cairns, *Christianity Through the Centuries* (Grand Rapids: Zondervan, 1981), pp. 301-08.
9. See J.W. Davidson, *The Logic of Millennial Thought* (New Haven: Yale University Press, 1977), pp. 280-97.
10. On the history of Miller and the Adventists, see G.J. Paxton, *The Shaking of Adventism* (Grand Rapids: Eerdmans, 1962).
11. On the history of Russell and the Jehovah's Witnesses, see W.R. Martin, *The Kingdom of the Cults* (Minneapolis: Bethany Fellowship, 1965), pp. 34-110.
12. For a discussion of the views of Herbert and Garner Ted Armstrong, see J. Hopkins, *The Armstrong Empire* (Grand Rapids: Eerdmans, 1974).
13. Representatives of postmillennial eschatology include Loraine Boettner, *The Millennium* (Philadelphia: Presbyterian and Reformed, 1957); J.M. Kik, *An Eschatology of Victory* (Philadelphia: Presbyterian and Reformed, 1971); and R.J. Rushdoony, *Thy Kingdom Come* (Fairfax, VA: Thoburn Press, 1978).
14. Representatives of amillennial eschatology include G.C. Berkouwer, *The Return of Christ* (Grand Rapids: Eerdmans, 1962); P.E. Hughes, *Interpreting Prophecy* (Grand Rapids: Eerdmans, 1976); and A. Hoekema, *The Bible and the Future* (Grand Rapids: Eerdmans, 1979).
15. Representatives of premillennial eschatology include H.A. Hoyt, *The End Times* (Chicago: Moody Press, 1969); Rene Pache, *The Return of Jesus*

Christ (Chicago: Moody Press, 1955); J.D. Pentecost, *Things to Come* (Grand Rapids: Zondervan, 1958); and John F. Walvoord, *Major Bible Prophecies* (Grand Rapids: Zondervan, 1991).

16. See J.F. Walvoord, *The Blessed Hope and the Tribulation* (Grand Rapids: Zondervan, 1975); H.L. Willmington, *The King Is Coming* (Wheaton: Tyndale House, 1973); Thomas Ice and Timothy Demy, eds., *When the Trumpet Sounds* (Eugene, OR: Harvest House, 1995); W.R. Willis and J.R. Master, eds., *Issues in Dispensationalism* (Chicago: Moody Press, 1994).

17. See J.O Buswell, *A Systematic Theology of the Christian Religion* (Grand Rapids: Zondervan, 1962), vol. 2, pp. 393-450; and N.B. Harrison, *The End* (Minneapolis: Harrison, 1941).

18. See J.B. Payne, *The Imminent Appearing of Jesus Christ* (Grand Rapids: Eerdmans, 1962); G.E. Ladd, *The Blessed Hope* (Grand Rapids: Eerdmans, 1956); and R.H. Gundry, *The Church and the Tribulation* (Grand Rapids: Zondervan, 1973).

19. While both men lean toward amillennialism, neither has written extensively on the subject of eschatology.

20. Wycliffe's work on the pope was entitled *DePapa* (1379) and is included in H.E. Winn, ed., *Wycliff, Select English Writings* (Oxford: Oxford University Press, 1926), pp. 66-74. He wrote, "The Pope is antichrist heere in erth, for he is agens Christ bothe in lif and in lore."

21. This interpretation was first suggested by Otto of Freising (1111–1158) and Joachim of Fiore (1135–1202), with the dates readjusted by Sebastian Franck (1531) and John Carion (1532).

22. J. Owen, "Righteous Zeal Encouraged by Divine Protection" (January 31, 1649), in *Works of John Owen,* vol. VIII, pp. 128ff. Years later, in 1683, the University of Oxford condemned this sermon and ordered it burned. It was based on the text of Jeremiah 15:19,20; Owen compared Charles to Israel's King Manesseh.

23. This shift is generally credited to the influence of John Henry Alstead (1588–1638), Joseph Mede (1586–1638), and Thomas Goodwin (1600–1680). See E.E. Hindson, "The Growth of Apocalyptic Speculation in England 1588-1640" in *The Puritans' Use of Scripture in the Development of an Apocalyptical Hermeneutic* (Pretoria: University of South Africa, 1984), pp. 121-66.

24. See Ian Murray, *The Puritan Hope* (London: Banner of Truth, 1971); and J.W. Davidson, *The Logic of Millennial Thought: Eighteenth-Century New England* (New Haven: Yale University Press, 1977).

25. R.J. Rushdoony, *Institutes of Biblical Law*. For adaptations of his theory, see various issues of *The Journal of Christian Reconstruction*.

26. See G. Bahnsen, *By This Standard: The Authority of God's Law Today* (Fort Worth: Dominion Press, 1981).

27. Cited in Dobson and Hindson, "Apocalypse Now?", p. 20.
28. Quoted by R.C. Clapp, "Democracy As Heresy," in *Christianity Today* (February 20, 1987), pp. 17-24. His insightful criticism of postmillennial reconstructionism is most helpful.
29. R.J. Rushdoony, *By What Standard?* (Philadelphia: Presbyterian & Reformed, 1965).
30. G. North, *Unconditional Surrender* and *Backward Christian Soldiers? An Action Manual for Christian Reconstruction* (Tyler, TX: Institute for Christian Economics, 1984).
31. See R.G. Clouse, "Views of the Millennium," in W.A. Elwell, ed., *Evangelical Dictionary of Theology* (Grand Rapids: Baker, 1984), pp. 714-18.
32. Ibid.
33. J.N. Darby, *Collected Writings,* 34 vols. (Plymouth: Brethren Society). See W.A. Hoffecker, "Darby, John Nelson," in W.A. Elwell, ed., *Evangelical Dictionary of Theology* (Grand Rapids: Baker, 1984), pp. 292, 293.
34. C.I. Scofield, ed., *Scofield Reference Bible* (New York: Oxford University Press, 1909; new ed. 1917; 1967).
35. Tim LaHaye, *The Beginning of the End* (Wheaton, IL: Tyndale House, 1972).
36. This is a major belief of dispensationalism. See note 15 for references and sources.
37. See Jeremiah 30:5-7; Matthew 24:3-30; Daniel 12:1-3; Mark 13:19; Luke 21:23.
38. Quoted in Dobson and Hindson, "Apocalypse Now?", pp. 21, 22.
39. J.D. Pentecost, *Things to Come* (Grand Rapids: Zondervan, 1958), p. 275.
40. Harry Rimmer, *The Coming War and the Rise of Russia* (Grand Rapids: Eerdmans, 1940) and *The Shadow of Coming Events* (Grand Rapids: Eerdmans, 1946).
41. See Isaiah 43:5-7; Jeremiah 12:15; Ezekiel 20:42; Joel 3:1; Amos 9:14,15; Micah 4:6; Zechariah 10:10; Zephaniah 3:12,13; Romans 11:26,27.
42. Hal Lindsey, *The Late Great Planet Earth,* pp. 12ff.
43. See Hal Lindsey's *The Terminal Generation* (Santa Ana, CA: Vision House, 1975).
44. See also Matthew 24:43,44.
45. See Dobson and Hindson, "Apocalypse Now?", pp. 21,22.
46. Ibid.

Chapter 12: Is There Any Hope?

1. William Willimon, "The Chains of Religious Freedom," *Christianity Today* (September 18, 1987), pp. 28-30.
2. Ibid., p. 29.

3. This theme is developed by Tim LaHaye in chapter 1, "Help! We've Been Robbed," and chapter 2, "Who Secularized America?" in *Faith of Our Founding Fathers* (Nashville: Wolgemuth & Hyatt, 1987), pp. 1-29.

4. R.C. Sproul, *Lifeviews: Understanding the Ideas That Shape Society Today* (Old Tappan, NJ: Revell, 1986), p. 29.

5. Paul Johnson, "The Almost Chosen People," in Richard Neuhaus, ed., *Unsecular America* (Grand Rapids: Eerdmans, 1986), pp. 1-13.

6. This theme is repeated throughout Richard Neuhaus' *The Naked Public Square* (Grand Rapids: Eerdmans, 1984).

7. Ibid., p. 30.

8. Ibid., p. 37.

9. Ibid., pp. 216-21.

10. See Ed Hindson, "The Mainline Is Becoming the Sideline," *Religious Broadcasting* (February 1988), pp. 22-23.

11. Charles Colson, *Kingdoms in Conflict* (Grand Rapids: Zondervan, 1987), p. 304.

12. Richard Neuhaus, "Christian Monisms Against the Gospel," *Religion & Society Report* (September 1987), pp. 1-3.

13. John Stott, *Involvement: Being a Responsible Christian in a Non-Christian Society* (Old Tappan, NJ: Revell, 1984), pp. 34-36.

14. See Robert Webber, *The Church and the World* (Grand Rapids: Zondervan, 1986), pp. 81-142.

15. Ibid., p. 121.

16. John Calvin, *Institutes of the Christian Religion* (Philadelphia: Westminster Press, 1960), 4:20.2.

17. Tim LaHaye, "Response," in Elwood McQuaid, "What's Left for the Religious Right?" *Moody Monthly* (February 1988), pp. 12-17.

18. Michael Green, *I Believe in Satan's Downfall* (Grand Rapids: Eerdmans, 1981), p. 209.

19. Ibid., p. 213.

20. Ibid., p. 214.

21. Donald Grey Barnhouse, *The Invisible War* (Grand Rapids: Zondervan, 1965), p. 230.

22. Ibid., pp. 232-33.

23. Erwin Lutzer, *The Serpent of Paradise* (Chicago: Moody Press, 1996), p. 186.

Bibliography

Anderson, Robert. *The Coming Prince*. London: Hodder & Stoughton, 1894.

Andrews, Samuel. *Christianity and Antichristianity*. Chicago: Moody Bible Institute, 1898.

Couch, Mal, ed., *Dictionary of Premillennial Theology*. Grand Rapids: Kregel, 1996.

Dobson, Ed. *The End*. Grand Rapids: Zondervan, 1997.

Froese, Arno. *How Democracy Will Elect the Antichrist*. Columbia, SC: The Olive Press, 1997.

Hindson, Ed. *Approaching Armageddon*. Eugene, OR: Harvest House, 1997.

———. *Final Signs*. Eugene, OR: Harvest House, 1996.

Hoyt, Herman. *The End Times*. Chicago: Moody Press, 1969.

Hunt, Dave. *A Woman Rides the Beast*. Eugene, OR: Harvest House, 1994.

Ice, Thomas and Timothy Demy. *Fast Facts on Bible Prophecy*. Eugene, OR: Harvest House, 1997.

———. *Prophecy Watch*. Eugene, OR: Harvest House, 1998.

James, William, ed., *Foreshocks of Antichrist*. Eugene, OR: Harvest House, 1997.

Jeffrey, Grant. *Prince of Darkness*. Toronto: Frontier Research Publications, 1994.

LaHaye, Tim. *No Fear of the Storm*. Sisters, OR: Multnomah Press, 1992.

Lalonde, Peter. *One World Under Antichrist*. Eugene, OR: Harvest House, 1991.

Pentecost, J. Dwight. *Things to Come*. Grand Rapids: Zondervan, 1965.

Pink, Arthur W. *The Antichrist*. Minneapolis: Klock & Klock, 1979.

Price, Walter. *The Coming Antichrist*. Chicago: Moody Press, 1974.

Walvoord, John F. *Major Bible Prophecies*. Grand Rapids: Zondervan, 1991.

About the Author

Ed Hindson is the assistant pastor of the 9,000-member Rehoboth Baptist Church in Atlanta, Georgia, and vice-president of "There's Hope!" ministries. He is also professor of religion and dean of the Institute of Biblical Studies at Liberty University in Lynchburg, Virginia. An executive board member of the Pre-Trib Research Center in Washington, D.C., Hindson is also a Life Fellow of the International Biographical Association of Cambridge, England. The degrees Hindson holds are: B.A., William Tyndale College; M.A., Trinity Evangelical Divinity School; Th.M., Grace Theological Seminary; Th.D., Trinity Graduate School; D.Min., Westminster Theological Seminary; D.Phil., University of South Africa. He has also done graduate study at Acadia University in Nova Scotia, Canada.

Hindson has served as a visiting lecturer at both Oxford University and the Harvard Divinity School, as well as numerous evangelical seminaries including Dallas, Denver, Trinity, Grace, and Westminster. He has taught over 30,000 students in the past 30 years. His solid academic scholarship combined with a dynamic and practical teaching style communicate biblical truth in a powerful and positive manner. His books include: *Angels of Deceit, End Times and the New World Order, Approaching Armageddon,* and *Final Signs.* He also served as general editor of the King James Study Bible and the *Parallel Bible Commentary,* and was one of the translators for the New King James Version.

Other Good
Harvest House Reading

Approaching Armaggeddon
Ed Hindson

Is there more than one judgment? Who is the Antichrist? What signs should we watch for as we speed toward end times? *Approaching Armaggeddon* sheds light on God's answers found in the book of Revelation, illuminates the urgency of accepting Jesus Christ, and prepares you with a "big picture" of the times to come.

Final Signs
Ed Hindson

Ed Hindson offers fast-moving, intriguing background on more than two dozen of the most amazing prophecies in Scripture, including the establishment of a world government, the rapture of the church, and the rise of the Antichrist and the False Prophet.

Totally Sufficient
Ed Hindson

Experts in the fields of counseling, science, and ministry explore the reasons why the Bible holds all the answers to your questions about life and faith. Insights from this book will help you minister to fellow Christians who are finding it difficult to rely on God in their times of trial and need.

Occult Invasion
Dave Hunt

Occult influences flow freely in America today, seeping into our homes, schools, and churches. How can we as Christians recognize what comes from the occult? Noted cult and prophecy expert Dave Hunt exposes how the occult is invading our world through spirit communications, UFOs, hypnosis, holistic health, and "Christian" psychology practices.

Alien Obsession
Ron Rhodes

What is the real message of UFOs? What lies behind the abductions, the sightings, and the mysteries? This book will challenge you to carefully examine the UFO phenomenon in light of the eternal truth of God's Word.